Reading Through History

History Brief:

The 90s & The 2000s

By Jake Henderson

Other History Brief books:

The Age of Explorers
The American Colonies
The American Revolution
Early American History
The Roaring Twenties
The Great Depression
Oklahoma History
African Americans
The 70s & 80s
Halloween
Christmas

The 90s & 2000s
by Jake Henderson
©2019

ISBN-13: 9781797656076

Reading Through History
Woodward, OK, USA

Table of Contents:

(Continued on Next Page)

Table of Contents (Continued):

The 1992 Presidential Election

George HW Bush ran for re-election in 1992. Who ran against him? What was the result?

Following a successful outcome to the Persian Gulf War in 1991, President George HW Bush was incredibly popular. His approval rating amongst the American people was well over 80%, meaning that over 80% of the nation thought he was doing a good job as president.

However, an economic recession throughout 1992 damaged the president's popularity. Also, in 1988, Bush had famously promised that there would be "no new taxes." This promise could not be kept and taxes had increased. Despite this, as the sitting president, Bush was easily able to secure the Republican nomination in 1992 and seek a second term.

Nearly a dozen Democrats were interested in challenging

the incumbent. Early primaries included former Massachusetts Senator Paul Tsongas, California governor Jerry Brown, and Senator Bob Kerrey of Nebraska. However, it was the Governor of Arkansas, Bill Clinton, who emerged as the frontrunner.

Clinton managed to overcome a scandal early in the primaries, in which he was accused of having an inappropriate relationship with a woman named Gennifer Flowers. After putting the scandal behind him, Clinton went on to win thirty-five states throughout the primaries. He was officially named the Democratic nominee at the Democratic National Convention in July of 1992. He selected Al Gore, a senator from Tennessee, as his vice presidential running mate.

Bill Clinton   *George HW Bush*

The 1992 presidential election also saw the emergence of a third-party candidate. Ross Perot, a billionaire from Texas, announced on February 20th, 1992, that he would seek the presidency as an independent. Perot proved to be a popular candidate amongst many Republicans who were frustrated with George Bush over economic issues.

As the race went on, Bush campaigned against Clinton's character issues. He also argued that Clinton lacked the military experience necessary to be the commander-in-chief. However, Clinton continued to attract younger voters. Many saw him as an invigorating and refreshing choice. Clinton made appearances on late-night television talk show programs, wore sunglasses, and played the saxophone. By comparison, Bush seemed out-of-touch and old-fashioned.

When voters went to the polls in November, Clinton emerged victorious, winning 43% of the popular vote to Bush's 37.5%. Ross Perot had a significant impact, garnering nearly 19% of the popular vote. In the Electoral College, Clinton won thirty-two states, accumulating 370 electoral votes. Bush received 168 electoral votes, while Ross Perot finished with none.

The 1992 election was significant in many regards. Because of Clinton's victory, presidential candidates were expected to be younger and more energetic. They also began making an effort to be more entertaining, reaching out to the public with increased television appearances.

The 1992 election is also thought of as a "realigning" election. The all-important state of California had voted

Republican in every presidential election from 1952 through 1988. However, Clinton's victory in that state in 1992 would firmly place California as a Democratic state. Also, Southern states, which had once solidly supported Democrats, continued to shift towards the Republican Party.

*President Bill Clinton walks with
Vice President Al Gore*

Bill Clinton

Bill Clinton became the 42nd President of the United States in 1992. Where was Bill Clinton from? What did he do before becoming president?

Bill Clinton was born in Hope, Arkansas on August 19th, 1946. His given name was William Jefferson Blythe III. His father died in car accident three months before he was born. In 1950, Clinton's mother married Roger Clinton. Bill assumed the last name Clinton when he was fifteen years old.

As a high school student, Clinton was a talented musician, playing the saxophone in the Hot Springs High School band. After graduating, he attended Georgetown University where he received a degree in Foreign Service. He was then awarded a Rhodes Scholarship to University College, Oxford, in the United Kingdom. After one year, he chose instead to attend Yale Law School and returned to the United States.

Bill Clinton with his wife, Hillary

Throughout his college experience, Clinton was an outspoken critic of the Vietnam Conflict. He participated in protests and refused to volunteer to serve in the military. He did register for the draft but went undrafted. His open opposition to the war led many to label him as a "draft dodger" throughout his political career.

During his time at Yale, he met Hillary Rodham in 1971. The two dated for several years before marrying in October of 1975. The couple would eventually have a daughter, Chelsea, who was born in 1980.

Following his graduation from Yale Law School, Clinton briefly served as a professor of law at the University of Arkansas. In 1974, he ran an unsuccessful campaign for the House of Representatives. Two years later, he ran unopposed to become the Attorney General of Arkansas.

In 1978, Clinton was elected as the Governor of Arkansas. At the time, he was only 32 years old, making him the youngest governor in the nation. In his first re-election bid in 1980, Clinton was defeated by the Republican candidate Frank White. Clinton ran for governor once more in 1982 and was elected again. This time, he would maintain his role as governor of Arkansas for ten years, winning re-election in 1984, 1986, and 1990.

As the governor of Arkansas, Clinton worked to improve the state's education system. He also reduced state taxes for senior citizens. During this time, Clinton also served as the Chairman of the National Governors Association from 1986 to 1987. Throughout the late 1980s, he became a visible, national figure, even speaking at the 1988 Democratic National Convention, introducing Michael Dukakis as the

Democratic nominee.

In 1992, Bill Clinton became the Democratic nominee for president. He competed against the Republican incumbent George HW Bush and independent Ross Perot. Clinton emerged victorious, becoming the 42nd President of the United States.

Throughout the 1990s, efforts made by the Clinton Administration reduced the federal deficit and helped the government operate on a more balanced budget. This means that the government was making a concentrated effort to not spend more money than it had available to it. During the Clinton presidency, the Congressional Budget Office reported surpluses in 1998, 1999, and 2000.

Clinton oversaw several military campaigns while he was commander-in-chief. In 1993, the Battle of Mogadishu saw the deaths of eighteen US soldiers, seventy-three more soldiers being wounded, and two helicopters being shot down. The United States also played a role in the Yugoslav Wars, both in Bosnia in 1995 and Kosovo in 1999.

During Clinton's time in office, his administration was plagued by many scandals. Amongst the more prominent was the Whitewater Scandal which involved questionable real estate investments made by the Clintons during the 1980s. An additional scandal involved rumors that Clinton, while governor, had used highway patrolmen to procure women for romantic encounters with him. This scandal became known as "Troopergate." Clinton was also sued by a woman named Paula Jones, who claimed he had sexually harassed her while he was the Governor of Arkansas.

However, the scandal his administration will most be

remembered for involved a young intern named Monica Lewinsky. Lewinsky was a 22-year-old who worked in the White House. President Clinton became involved in an inappropriate relationship with Miss Lewinsky. While under investigation, Clinton lied about the nature of this relationship while under oath. His statements eventually led to his impeachment by the House of Representatives. In December of 1998, he became only the second president in the history of the United States to be impeached. However, the Senate did not convict him, and, as a result, he was allowed to remain in office.

Clinton also received heavy criticism for issuing 141 pardons during his final days in office. Amongst the most controversial was the pardoning of Marc Rich. It was believed that Hillary Clinton's brother, Hugh Rodham, had accepted payments for convincing Bill to pardon Rich.

Bill Clinton helped to change the nature of the presidency. His charm and charisma played a large part in his election. As a result, presidential candidates are expected to be not only good politicians but highly-polished television personalities as well.

After serving two terms as president, Clinton remained very active. He frequently gave speeches and raised funds on behalf of the Democratic Party. He was also not afraid to voice his opinions when he disagreed with the direction taken by one of his successors. When needed, Clinton also served as an ambassador, traveling to locations such as North Korea where he negotiated on behalf of the US to help secure the release of two American journalists who had been captured.

The Branch Davidians

In the spring of 1993, an incident occurred in Waco, Texas. What happened? What impact did it have on society?

Sometime around 1930, a schism occurred within the Seventh-day Adventist Church. This schism resulted in Victor Houteff being removed from the Seventh Day Adventist Church and forming a new a religious sect. This new sect, which eventually became known as the Branch Davidians, settled just west of Waco, Texas in 1935. The Branch Davidians established a facility there known as Mount Carmel Center.

In 1990, this small religious group fell under the leadership of David Koresh (whose given name was Vernon Wayne Howell). Through Koresh's teachings, the Branch Davidians became convinced of an approaching apocalypse. As a result, the group began stockpiling a large supply of weapons in preparation for this event.

The group's activities drew the attention of the Bureau of Alcohol, Tobacco, and Firearms (ATF). The ATF began investigating the Branch Davidians for possible weapons violations (It was suspected that it was unlawful for civilians to own many of the weapons in their possession). As a result, a warrant to search the Mount Carmel Compound was obtained by ATF agents.

On February 28th, 1993, seventy-six agents from the ATF approached Mount Carmel Center with the intention of searching the facility and arresting David Koresh. As the agents approached, those inside the compound opened fire. In the ensuing gun battle, four AFT officers were killed and sixteen more were wounded. Six Branch Davidians were also killed and several others were wounded.

Following this exchange, the ATF agents laid siege to the compound, not allowing anyone in or out of the facility. The bureau agents patrolled the perimeter of the property with tanks and Bradley Fighting Vehicles. They played loud noises such as jet engines and heavy metal music to prevent the Branch Davidians from sleeping. They also shot holes in the compound's water towers to deprive them of hydration.

The siege lasted for fifty-one days. During that time, negotiations took place between Koresh and the Federal Bureau of Investigation (FBI). The FBI did successfully negotiate for the release of nineteen children, but many more stayed inside the compound.

On April 19th, 1993, the siege came to an end. Agents from the ATF and FBI advanced towards the compound with armored vehicles, tear gas, and flash grenades. During the raid, the compound caught fire. As a result of the blaze, seventy-six Branch Davidians were killed (nine survived). To this day, numerous questions remain about how the fires began. Government officials claim the Branch Davidians started the fires. Others claim that the fires started accidentally, while still others say that the government agents ignited the fires.

When the compound was finally searched, over two hundred separate weapons were discovered. Amongst the weapons found were 40 sub-machine guns, 54 AK-47s, hand grenades, a rocket-propelled grenade launcher, and parts to build rocket-propelled grenades.

The Branch Davidian incident has been used by many as an example of the US government becoming too powerful and too intrusive into the lives of US citizens. Many who oppose the government view the attack on the Branch Davidians as both a violation of the First Amendment right to freedom of religion and the Second Amendment right to bear arms.

One individual who took his resentment of the US Government to the extreme was Tim McVeigh, the perpetrator of the Oklahoma City bombing. He chose the Alfred P. Murrah Federal Building in Oklahoma City as a target because he incorrectly believed that the agents responsible for the Branch Davidian incident were stationed there. Furthermore, he chose the date of April 19th for his 1995 attack to coincide with the date of the second Waco raid. One hundred and sixty-eight people died as a result of McVeigh's actions.

Many also support the actions of the US government,

stating that the Branch Davidians were a potentially dangerous group and that the federal agencies took the necessary steps to bring the situation to a conclusion. Either way, it is certain that the Branch Davidian incident will linger in the nation's memory for years to come.

David Koresh, leader of the Branch Davidians

The Battle of Mogadishu

In 1993, the Battle of Mogadishu occurred. Why did the Battle of Mogadishu happen? What were the results?

The president of Somalia, Mohammed Siad Barre, was overthrown by opposing clans in January of 1991. These various groups then began fighting each other as they competed for political control of the country. This conflict became known as the Somali Civil War. Throughout 1991 and 1992, this war caused thousands of deaths and damaged the nation's agricultural production. As a result, thousands more starved to death. It has been estimated that approximately 300,000 Somalis died in 1991 and 1992 as a result of the war or starvation.

The United Nations (UN) attempted to provide relief to the people of Somalia by airlifting aid to remote areas of the country. More than 48,000 tons of food and medical supplies were flown into the region. Unfortunately for the

Somalians, many of these supplies were captured by the warring clan leaders. The leaders traded the supplies to other nations in exchange for weapons to continue their war. This, in turn, caused even more suffering and starvation within the war-torn country.

As part of the UN peace-keeping efforts in Somalia, the United States deployed troops to the region. In August of 1993, President Bill Clinton authorized the creation of a task force made up of special operations units from the Army, Air Force, and Navy. The force included more than 400 Army Rangers and members of the US Army's elite Delta Force.

On October 3rd, 1993, this task force conducted an operation which was intended to capture Mohamed Farrah Aidid, the leader of one of these warring clans, and a number of his high-ranking officers. The mission involved 160 men, twelve vehicles, and nineteen aircraft.

As the assault began, Somali fighters shot down two Black Hawk helicopters over the capital city of Mogadishu. The crashing of the helicopters in a war zone created a desperate situation for those who survived the impact. Mobs of locals and Somali militiamen began attempting to overrun the crash sites. Some of the wounded were evacuated in the remaining Black Hawks, but others were trapped in the wreckage or too badly injured to escape.

At the first crash site, both pilots died as a result of the impact, while two of the crew chiefs were critically wounded. Those who were able to defend the site found themselves trapped in a hostile environment for the remainder of the day and into the following morning. The soldiers were forced to build makeshift shelters out of Kevlar armor plates and engage in urban warfare until a rescue convoy arrived at 1:55 AM on October 4th.

At the second crash site, Delta snipers Randy Shughart and Gary Gordon requested to be inserted from a third Black Hawk to defend their wounded comrades until help arrived. While their first two requests were denied, the snipers were eventually granted permission. As they defended the site, their own Black Hawk was hit with an RPG and forced to withdraw. Shughart and Gordon refused to be evacuated, and both men remained by their comrades' sides. During the night, a mob numbering in the thousands overran the location, killing the snipers and all but one of the survivors of the original crew. The lone survivor, pilot Michael Durant, was dragged into the street and nearly beaten to death before being taken hostage by members of Aidid's militia.

The crew of one of the Blackhawk helicopters
shot down over Mogadishu

The Battle of Mogadishu came to a conclusion after survivors and defenders of the first crash site were able to rendezvous with an armored rescue convoy. During the evacuation, many Ranger and Delta Force soldiers were forced to travel on foot as the vehicles were filled with the bodies of the dead and wounded. As the convoy moved, it faced constant gunfire and attack from rocket-propelled grenades. This arduous event has become known as the Mogadishu Mile. The convoy eventually reached safety at Mogadishu Stadium, and the soldiers were extracted from the city.

The Battle of Mogadishu resulted in the deaths of 19 American soldiers, with an additional 73 wounded and one pilot taken hostage. It is estimated that over 300 Somalis died and more than 800 were wounded.

Television images of Somalis dragging the bodies of dead US soldiers through the streets outraged the American public, which became highly critical of the event. The Battle of Mogadishu had been the bloodiest battle involving US troops since the Vietnam Conflict. The mission was viewed by most as a dismal failure, and the Clinton Administration received heavy criticism because of the event. This backlash eventually led to Les Aspin, the US Secretary of Defense, resigning and accepting blame for the disaster.

Following the incident, President Clinton ordered a halt to all military action against the forces of Mohamed Farrah Aidid, except those required in self-defense. The United States also reduced the amount of humanitarian aid it sent to the war-torn country, and the incident is cited as one of the primary reasons for the US military not intervening in future Conflicts in Africa, such as the Rwandan Genocide of 1994.

In 1999, Black Hawk Down was published by Mark Bowden. This book relays the events surrounding the Battle of Mogadishu. In 2001, a film version of Black Hawk Down was also released to high acclaim.

In 2003, Black Hawk pilot Michael Durant, who was captured and held hostage for eleven days, published In the Company of Heroes, which describes his experiences. For their heroic roles in helping to save Durant's life, Delta snipers Randy Shughart and Gary Gordon both received the Medal of Honor posthumously.

The Oklahoma City Bombing

In the spring of 1995, a catastrophe occurred in Oklahoma City. What happened that day? Who was responsible?

At 9:02 AM, on April 19th, 1995, a tremendous explosion shook Oklahoma City. Glass, granite, concrete, and steel rained down from the sky around the Alfred P. Murrah Federal Building. The blast was so powerful that street signs and parking meters had been ripped from the ground. Pedestrians were lifted off their feet and thrown across the sidewalk. Glass had been shattered in windows several blocks away.

The Murrah Building was almost completely destroyed. The devastation inside was horrific and survival was determined only by where an individual happened to be in the building at the time of the blast. The upper floors had collapsed upon the lower ones, leaving little chance for anyone on the ground level.

Rescue workers rushed to the scene and began searching for survivors. The work was dangerous due to the possibility that the rest of the building could collapse. However, rescue crews worked quickly to ensure that more lives would not be lost. By the time the rescue operations were complete, 168 deaths (including 19 children) had been recorded, and more than 500 had been wounded.

Americans from across the nation journeyed to Oklahoma City to volunteer their time and energy. Eventually, more than 12,000 people would participate in the rescue efforts, humanitarian aid, and cleanup effort that would follow. Others found different ways to assist the cause. Donations of bottled water, helmets, lights, wheelbarrows, and other equipment came pouring in. Thousands of meals were also donated and served to relief workers by charitable organizations. Also, more than 9,000 units of blood were donated by Oklahomans and others around the country in response to requests for blood donations.

Many Americans also made financial donations. More than $40 million was donated to help the families of those who died, or were severely wounded that day. $18 million of this was set aside to provide for college educations for the 219 children who lost at least one parent in this tragedy.

While rescue workers searched for survivors, investigative teams were attempting to discover the cause of the explosion. Within minutes, the authorities realized that the source of the blast had been a 4,800 pound ammonium-nitrate bomb which had been hidden inside a Ryder truck.

At first, the investigators suspected the work of Middle East terrorists. Unfortunately, the eventual truth proved to be even more frightening. It was soon announced that the primary culprit was an American veteran named Tim McVeigh. He had been arrested in Perry, Oklahoma on an unrelated concealed weapons charge. He was in jail, awaiting arraignment when it was revealed that he was the primary suspect in the bombing investigation.

*Tim McVeigh, alongside the police sketch
of who authorities were searching for.*

A US Army veteran of the Persian Gulf War, McVeigh was also a firearms enthusiast who enjoyed the outdoors and hunting. While in the military he had met Terry Nichols and Michael Fortier, the two men who became his co-conspirators in the bombing.

In 1993, the Bureau of Alcohol, Tobacco & Firearms had conducted a military-style siege of a compound owned by a religious group known as the Branch Davidians in Waco, Texas. McVeigh and Nichols saw this action as an infringement of civil liberties, so they devised a plan to retaliate. They had chosen the federal building in Oklahoma City as their target because they mistakenly believed that the ATF agents responsible for the raid were stationed there.

The bombing was largely planned and carried out by McVeigh and Nichols. They paid for, and collected the explosive materials. They also constructed the bomb, consulting instructions from bomb-making manuals. However, they relayed their plans to Fortier, and his wife Lori. Even though the couple was aware of the plot, neither one contacted authorities to prevent it from happening.

McVeigh, Nichols, and Fortier were all arrested and placed on trial for their involvement in the bombing of the Murrah Federal Building. Michael Fortier received 12 years in prison for his limited involvement in the plan. Terry Nichols was sentenced to life in prison, while Tim McVeigh was sentenced to death. McVeigh's sentence was carried out on June 11, 2001. He was the first prisoner to be executed by the federal government since 1963.

Bill Gates and Microsoft

Throughout the 1980s and 1990s, Bill Gates played a key role in developing the modern age. What did Bill Gates do? What impact has he had on society?

Bill Gates was born on October 28th, 1955, in Seattle, Washington. He became fascinated by computers in the eighth grade and began working with a local computer company to learn more about coding and the various programs that allowed the computers to function. Before he was out of high school, he had designed a payroll program for one company and had devised a program for his school district which helped enroll students in classes.

He graduated from high school in 1973 as a National Merit Scholar and scored 1590 (out of 1600) on the Scholastic Aptitude Test (SAT). He enrolled at Harvard and briefly studied to become a lawyer. However, after only two years at Harvard, he left to start his own computer software company.

Gates and his business partner Paul Allen named the

company Micro-Soft (eventually Microsoft), and the small business began to develop programming language software for various computer systems. In 1980, IBM approached Microsoft about developing an operating system for IBM's upcoming personal computer (PC). Microsoft purchased an operating system from a smaller company and presented it to IBM, which used it in their new PCs. This operating system became known as the Microsoft Disk Operating System, or MS-DOS.

Throughout the 1980s and 1990s, Microsoft continued to become a more powerful presence in the world of computer software. The company helped to revolutionize the personal computer with operating systems such as Windows as well as browsing programs such as Internet Explorer.

As Microsoft became a successful company, Gates' wealth continued to grow. At the age of 32, he became a billionaire. In 1995, he became the wealthiest person on the planet, a title which he held for twelve years. At one point, in 1999, his wealth exceeded $101 billion.

Gates has donated considerable amounts of his money to philanthropic endeavors. In 2000, he and his wife established the Bill & Melinda Gates Foundation. This is a charitable organization that supports many different causes and is amongst the wealthiest charitable organizations in the world today. In 2010, Gates, along with his wife Melinda, vowed to give away more than half of their wealth to charitable endeavors.

Gates' impact on the world is difficult to calculate. The innovations developed by the Microsoft Corporation have revolutionized both home and office computing. Aside from the financial success that Microsoft experienced, there have been many other businesses which have prospered due to using Microsoft products.

A personal computer in nearly every home, office, and classroom has become a reality. Bill Gates played a major role in making this reality possible. For this reason, he will continue to be viewed as a historical figure that helped to shape the modern era.

Bill Gates

The Internet and the World Wide Web

In the 1990s, the internet was becoming an increasingly common part of day-to-day life. Where did the internet come from? How long has it existed?

In the early 1960s, researchers began experimenting with the notion of connecting computers at different locations. One such project was funded by the US Department of Defense and was known as the Advanced Research Project Agency Network (ARPANET). On October 29th, 1969, the first ARPANET link was established between the Stanford Research Institute and the University of California, Los Angeles (UCLA). On December 5th, two more schools were added to the network, the University of California, Santa Barbara and the University of Utah. By the end of 1971, there were fifteen different sites connected by ARPANET.

Throughout the 1970s and early 1980s, ARPANET continued to expand. However, since this computer network was government funded, it could not be used for commercial purposes. Also, access to it was restricted to military installations and universities. Eventually, this access was broadened to include more schools as well as a few businesses that were directly participating in the research of the technology.

As time progressed, more networks began developing as well. Other organizations, in various countries, had been working on similar technologies. Even though these other computer networks worked slightly differently, they all served the same basic function. Eventually, there were many different networks, and it was decided to merge these networks into one.

Other US government agencies became involved in the development of the technology. The National Science Foundation, the Department of Energy, and the National Aeronautics and Space Administration (NASA) all played a role in advancing the work which had been started by the Department of Defense's Advanced Research Project Agency.

The internet was opened to the public for commercial use in 1989. As the 1980s gave way to the 1990s, Americans, and people all over the world, began using the internet to access the World Wide Web. Throughout the 1990s, using the internet became more and more commonplace.

Many more families began purchasing home computers, and electronic mail (e-mail) slowly began to replace the pen and paper method of communication. Businesses developed their own websites, boasting their web address in television and radio commercials. More and more people began going "online" to consume news and make purchases.

The growth of the internet was not without its difficulties, however. From 1997 to 2001, many people began financially investing in "dot-com" companies. These were businesses that operated almost exclusively online. Sure that these businesses were the wave of the future, investors sunk large amounts of money into these dot-com companies. This became known as the "dot-com bubble." Unfortunately for these investors, the bubble burst when many of these companies failed and went out of business.

The internet has had a profound impact on the world. It has made communication, commerce, and business easier than ever before. It has also provided a source of news and entertainment for countless people. It has brought the world closer together and helped to create a global community. It has been estimated that, in the modern world (2018), there are more than three billion internet users, a number which grows every single day.

Daily Life and Popular Culture in the 1990s

The 1990s were an interesting time in America. What new items were people enjoying during the decade? What did Americans do for entertainment?

The American family looked increasingly different as the decade progressed. While there were many families that fit the traditional mold of a mother, father, and children, many less traditional types of families were becoming commonplace. Single-parent families became common, and many children had a stepmother or stepfather, or both, as divorced parents remarried.

The concept of the "stay-at-home mother" had nearly become a thing of the past, as both parents worked out of necessity to make ends meet and provide additional income for the family. At the beginning of the decade, the average income was close to $29,000, while at the end of the decade it had risen to more than $40,000. Of course, a person's income would vary depending on their chosen profession.

The price of a new car in 1990 was about $16,000. By the

end of the decade, the price had risen to $21,100. Of course, the price someone paid was largely determined by the make and model of the vehicle. Some prices actually went down as the decade progressed. For example, in 1990, a gallon of gas cost $1.34, while in 1999, a gallon of gas cost $1.22.

The average price of a postage stamp in the 1990s was 30 cents, a loaf of bread cost $1.50, and a gallon of milk cost $2.29. A nice leather jacket might have cost someone about $100, while a new video game system sold for about $160. Many of these prices would have varied from one region of the country to another.

Throughout the 1990s, several pieces of technology became increasingly common for American families. The cell phone (or mobile phone as they were called at the time) became an everyday sight in many larger cities. However, by the end of the decade, only about 28% of all Americans had a cell phone.

The personal computer became increasingly common in homes as well. Personal computers had been available since the late 1970s, but new operating systems in the 1990s, such as Windows 3.1 and Windows 95, made the computer more user-friendly. Before long, parents were keeping track of their finances and students were typing their homework on their home computer. In 1989, the "world wide web" was opened for commercial public use. As the decade progressed, most Americans got their first glimpse of the Internet. By the year 2000, it was estimated that there were 295 million Internet users worldwide.

Television continued to be a favorite form of family entertainment. Family sitcoms were still popular, just as they were in the 1980s. *Full House, Home Improvement, Rosanne*, and *The Simpsons* were amongst the most popular. However, as most families had more than one television, TV shows became increasingly focused towards certain demographics. For example, adults might have been watching *Seinfeld, ER*, or *Murphy Brown*. Whereas, teenagers might have been in the next room enjoying *Friends, Beverly Hills 90210*, or *Beavis & Butthead*.

Movies also played a dominant role in the entertainment industry throughout the 1990s. Animated films experienced a renaissance, as Disney saw box office success with *Beauty & the Beast, Aladdin*, and *The Lion King*. In 1995, Pixar released *Toy Story*, the first feature-length computer-animated film. This innovative film helped to revolutionize not only animated films, but live-action films and video games as well. In June of 1993, director Steven Spielberg kept audiences on the edge of their seats with *Jurassic Park*, and then in November, he delivered the powerful Holocaust drama *Schindler's List*. *The Silence of the Lambs* and *Pulp Fiction* were other films that captured the country's attention.

Most American families enjoyed following professional sports in the 1990s. Major League Baseball suffered in popularity because the players went on strike in 1994. The strike began in August of 1994, which meant there was no post-season play and no World Series that season. The strike did not end until the spring of 1995, causing the 1995 season to begin nearly a month late.

On the field, the Atlanta Braves played in five World Series throughout the decade but won only one championship. The Braves were led by pitcher Greg Maddux, an eight-time all-star who won the Cy Young Award four times. In 1998, Americans were riveted by Mark McGwire and Sammy Sosa as they both chased the single season home run record. McGwire established the new record with 70 home runs while Sosa finished with 66.

Michael Jordan and his Chicago Bulls dominated the National Basketball Association (NBA) throughout the 1990s. The Bulls won the NBA championship six times, and Jordan was named the league's Most Valuable Player four times in the decade (an award he won five times in his career). For the first time, NBA players were allowed to participate in the Summer Olympics in 1992. The United States assembled a team of the best players the NBA had to offer and easily won the gold medal. This super team became known as the Dream Team.

The best team in the National Football League (NFL) throughout the 1990s was the Dallas Cowboys. Led by quarterback Troy Aikman, running back Emmitt Smith, and wide receiver Michael Irvin, the Cowboys won the Super Bowl in 1992, 1993, and 1996. The Buffalo Bills, led by Jim Kelly and Thurman Thomas, appeared in four consecutive Super Bowls but did not win a championship. John Elway, Brett Favre, and Barry Sanders were other extremely popular players throughout the decade.

In the world of music, Mariah Carey became one of the most popular singers of the decade, producing an impressive fourteen #1 songs. Throughout the decade, Carey sold approximately 97 million albums worldwide. Garth Brooks made country music popular throughout the nation. Brooks sold millions of albums and produced eighteen chart-topping songs, while another thirteen reached the top ten.

The sound that possibly defined the decade became known as "alternative rock" or grunge. This was a distinctive style of music that did not fit the constructs of pop music, rap, country, or any other genre. Pearl Jam, the Red Hot Chili Peppers, and Stone Temple Pilots were alternative groups who experienced considerable success. However, it was Nirvana that set the standard for alternative music. Led by Kurt Cobain, Nirvana became extraordinarily popular in the first half of the decade. Sadly, Cobain took his own life in April of 1994.

Fashion in the 1990s was molded by other cultural influences of the day. For example, alternative music performers popularized the "grunge" fashion trend of unkempt clothing and hair. Flannel, plaid shirts, and long hair also became popular. Styles worn by hip-hop artists were also common in the early part of the 1990s. By the end of the decade, fashion was trending more towards the stylish and glamorous. As with the fashion of any decade, the trends would largely be determined by what part of the country someone was living in and that individual's age at the time.

It should be remembered that not every family experienced the 1990s in the same way. These were just a few of the broad trends that were predominant throughout the decade. Each family and individual had a unique situation, with their own stories, tastes, and preferences.

Troy Aikman became one of the most successful and most popular athletes of the decade, playing quarterback for the Dallas Cowboys and leading them to three Super Bowl victories.

The Yugoslav Wars

During the 1990s, the United States, acting as a part of NATO, became involved in a conflict known as the Yugoslav Wars. Why were the Yugoslav Wars fought? How did these conflicts end?

The nation of Yugoslavia was created between World War I and World War II. It was made up of six smaller republics which included Macedonia, Slovenia, Montenegro, Bosnia and Herzegovina, Serbia, and Croatia. There were also two smaller provinces, Vojvodina and Kosovo, within Serbia.

In the late 1980s and early 1990s, as communism collapsed across Eastern Europe, a wave of nationalism swept across each of the Yugoslav republics. Each republic desired to be an independent country. On June 25th, 1991, Croatia and Slovenia both declared their independence from

Yugoslavia. In September of that same year, Macedonia declared its independence as well. On April 6th, 1992, Bosnia and Herzegovina was also recognized as an independent nation.

However, this separation was not without bloodshed. Beginning in 1991, the region that was once Yugoslavia began to see a considerable amount of warfare. This fighting would last for the remainder of the decade, up through 2001. This series of wars has collectively become known as the Yugoslav Wars.

Much of the fighting was based on ethnicity. Within each of these republics, large numbers of ethnic minorities from the other republics had settled in the region. For example, there were significant numbers of Serbians and Croatians living in Bosnia and Herzegovina. When Bosnia and Herzegovina declared its independence from Yugoslavia, fighting broke out between the Bosnians, Serbs, and Croats.

Similarly, in Kosovo, fighting occurred between Albanians living in Kosovo and Serbians who were attempting to remove them from the region. Tensions between these various groups had been building for years, but the Yugoslav army had always kept the different ethnic groups from actual warfare. As the separate republics declared their independence, the tensions boiled over into bloodshed.

Armed forces representing the North Atlantic Treaty Organization (NATO) helped bring the fighting to an end. NATO is a military alliance made up of the United States, the United Kingdom, France, and many other European and North American countries. NATO supplied more than 60,000 troops to Bosnia in order to bring peace to that region. NATO also deployed troops in 1998 to help bring an end to the situation in Kosovo, using extensive bombing which resulted in the deaths of more than 500 people.

There were many atrocities committed during the Yugoslav Wars. Thousands of innocent civilians died as the various ethnicities attempted to eliminate other groups from their region. During the Bosnian War, it is estimated that nearly 100,000 people were killed and more than two million were displaced from their homes. Serbs living in Bosnia were found guilty of ethnic cleansing. This means in addition to expelling and killing the ethnic minorities, the Serbs also destroyed their places of worship, cemeteries, and historical buildings. These crimes were primarily committed against a group known as the Bosniaks, who were Serbian-Muslims. Crimes were also committed against the Croats. However, the Croats were also found to be guilty of similar atrocities.

More than 12,000 deaths occurred in the Kosovo War, including more than 7,000 Albanians. Over 900,000 people were displaced from their homes. The president of Yugoslavia, Slobodan Milošević, was arrested and placed on trial for war crimes, including genocide and crimes against humanity. His trial ended without a verdict as he died in a jail cell in 2000.

Peace agreements were eventually reached between all warring parties. The Bosnian War ended after a lengthy negotiation throughout 1994 and 1995. The agreements finally reached were known as the Washington Agreement (which was negotiated in Washington DC) and the Dayton Agreement (which was brokered in Dayton, Ohio). The

Kosovo War was ended by the Kumanovo Agreement, which was signed in June of 1999 in Kumanovo, Macedonia.

Slobodan Milošević

The Impeachment of Bill Clinton

In December of 1998, President Bill Clinton was impeached. What were the circumstances surrounding his impeachment? What happened after he was impeached?

In 1994, an independent counsel, Ken Starr, was appointed to investigate the "Whitewater scandal." Whitewater was a questionable real estate development investment involving Bill and Hillary Clinton which took place while Bill was Governor of Arkansas. Through the process of his extensive investigation, Starr discovered evidence that President Clinton might have engaged in an inappropriate relationship with a 22-year-old White House intern named Monica Lewinsky.

The scandal first became a news story on January 17th, 1998. Matt Drudge, of the online news website The Drudge Report, reported the affair several days before any other news agency. Later that month, on January 21st, the

Washington Post reported it as well. Initially, the president denied the allegations, emphatically stating that he had not had a relationship with the young woman.

Speculation circulated throughout the year as details continued to be uncovered. It was revealed that the president and Miss Lewinsky had nine different encounters between 1995 and 1997. Lewinsky had confided the details of the relationship to a friend named Linda Tripp during telephone conversations. Tripp recorded the conversations and turned the tapes over to Starr.

On July 28th, 1998, Lewinsky testified before a grand jury regarding the nature of her relationship with the president. Finally, on August 17th, President Clinton addressed the nation, admitting to his indiscretions. However, in an earlier statement which Clinton had made while under oath, he had denied having a relationship with Miss Lewinsky. This false statement constituted perjury. Perjury (lying under oath) is punishable by law and is also an impeachable offense for federal officials.

In December of 1998, the House of Representatives brought four articles of impeachment against President Clinton. Impeachment is the process used by a legislative body to formally level charges against a high ranking official within the government. In the United States, this is a two part process. First, the House of Representatives must impeach the official. Then, the Senate conducts a trial to determine if the official will be removed from office based on the impeachment charges.

Two of the charges brought against Clinton related to the president committing perjury. Additional charges related to obstruction of justice and an abuse of power. One of the charges of perjury and the obstruction of justice charge passed the House of Representatives. The second charge of perjury and the abuse of power charge did not pass. With the passage of the two impeachment charges, Bill Clinton became only the second president in the history of the United States to be impeached. The first and only other was Andrew Johnson in 1868.

In February of 1999, the US Senate voted to acquit President Clinton of the charges against him. As a result, Clinton remained in office. Two months later, in a separate civil case related to the same issues, Clinton was found to be in contempt of court for providing misleading testimony and fined $90,000. Additionally, Clinton's license to practice law in the state of Arkansas was revoked.

The impeachment of President Clinton affected the nation for years to come. The political environment in Washington DC became increasingly partisan as the divide between Republicans and Democrats widened. Both parties, as well as the media, became focused on uncovering more scandals, and the entire event left a permanent blemish on the legacy of President Bill Clinton.

The US Senate in session during the trial of Bill Clinton

The Columbine School Massacre

In the spring of 1999, a tragedy occurred at Columbine High School, just outside of Littleton, Colorado. What happened that day? What were the long-term effects of the incident?

Eric Harris created a website in 1996. Initially, the purpose of the website related to the video game Doom, which Harris was a fan of. He created new levels of the game and allowed his friends to play them. Over time, he added a blog to his website. In this blog, he began expressing his frustrations about school, his classmates, and his parents. He also began sharing instructions about how to make pipe bombs and similar explosive devices.

Through this blog, he made several death threats against a classmate. The mother of this classmate learned about the threats and reported them to the sheriff's department. The sheriff's department discovered that Harris had also made violent threats against teachers and expressed a desire to kill many other people as well. However, law enforcement decided to not act on the evidence presented to them.

In late 1998, Harris and his close friend, Dylan Klebold, acquired several firearms through secondhand means. The two boys also spent considerable time constructing 99 explosive devices. Through journal entries and videos which were discovered later, the boys expressed their desire to commit an act of terrorism that would rival the 1995 bombing which had occurred in Oklahoma City.

On the morning of April 20th, 1999, Harris and Klebold placed two bombs, made from propane tanks, inside the school cafeteria. Their plan was to detonate the bombs and shoot students as they ran from the school. However, the bombs failed to detonate. Realizing their initial scheme had failed, the boys approached the building with firearms concealed beneath their coats.

At approximately 11:19 AM, they neared the cafeteria and opened fire on two students, Rachel Scott and Richard Castaldo, who were sitting on the grass outside. Harris and Klebold proceeded into the building, firing at will. Over the course of the next fifty minutes, the two terrorized the building, shooting students and teachers without remorse. They traversed the building, spending much of their time in the library. At approximately 12:08, Harris and Klebold turned the guns on themselves, bringing an end to their bloody spree. By the time it was over, the two had murdered thirteen people (twelve students and one teacher) and wounded an additional twenty-one.

The incident shocked the country. Immediately, the public began searching for answers, wondering what had caused Harris and Klebold to lash out in the manner they had. Some were quick to blame violent video games, movies, and music, which the two boys were fans of.

Others blamed America's obsession with firearms and the violent "gun culture" that had developed. In the aftermath of the Columbine incident, many new pieces of gun control legislation were proposed. Some of these measures included safety locks and banning the sale of high capacity ammunition magazines. Some retail outlets announced that they would no longer sell ammunition at all. Schools attempted to take proactive measures as well. Many districts began installing metal detectors and requiring students to carry see through backpacks. Numerous schools adopted "zero-tolerance" policies towards students who were in possession of weapons of any kind.

Students also began to see an increased number of security guards, as well as police officers permanently stationed on school grounds. "Intruder drills" and "school lock-down" procedures also became commonplace following this incident. Some communities even began participating in full scale practice drills, involving local police, fire departments, and other emergency responders.

School districts also began to place an emphasis on anti-bullying education. Harris and Klebold had frequently been mistreated by athletes in their school. During the attack, much of their attention was focused on those who had tormented them.

Columbine had a tradition of athletes wearing white ball caps. At one point during the assault, Harris and Klebold even demanded that all "guys in white hats" stand up. As a result, many districts began requiring students to wear school uniforms in hopes that cliques would be less likely to develop.

One additional result of the incident was an increased debate over whether young people should be prescribed anti-depressant medications. At the time of the assault, both boys were taking pharmaceutical medications to combat depression. The public began asking whether this type of violent behavior could be an unintended side effect of such drugs.

The tragedy which occurred at Columbine will always be remembered. The impact it had on society will be felt for many years to come. Schools and communities will undoubtedly continue to take preventive measures to ensure the safety of their students.

Members of a SWAT team participate in an "active shooter" drill.

The 2000 Presidential Election

In the year 2000, George W. Bush and Al Gore faced off in a historic presidential election. Who won this hard-fought contest? How close was the final vote?

As the year 2000 approached, President Bill Clinton was completing his second term. According to the Twenty-second Amendment, a president is only allowed to be elected to two terms. This meant he was ineligible to run for a third term, and new candidates would be seeking the office.

Clinton's vice president Al Gore was a logical choice to become the Democratic nominee. In the Democratic primary elections, Gore faced opposition from Bill Bradley, a senator from New Jersey. However, Bradley did not win a single state during the primaries. Bradley withdrew his candidacy on March 9, 2000, and Gore went on to become the Democratic nominee. Gore selected Senator Joe

Lieberman of Connecticut as his vice presidential running mate, and the two were officially nominated for the Democratic ticket on August 17, 2000, at the Democratic National Convention in Los Angeles, California.

On the Republican side, many candidates vied for the nomination, including Senator John McCain of Arizona, Ambassador Alan Keyes of Maryland, and businessman Steve Forbes of New Jersey. However, the early favorite was George W. Bush, the governor of Texas and son of former President George H.W. Bush. Bush's strongest opposition came from Senator McCain who won early primaries in New Hampshire, Michigan, and Arizona. However, Bush eventually pulled away to become the obvious choice for Republicans. Bush selected Dick Cheney, a former Secretary of Defense, as his vice presidential running mate, and the two formally accepted the Republican nomination on August 3, 2000, at the Republican National Convention in Philadelphia, Pennsylvania.

Aside from the two major parties, a number of third-party candidates also participated in the 2000 election. The Reform Party nominated Pat Buchanan, a writer and political commentator who had served as an advisor to President Richard Nixon. The Green Party chose Ralph Nader as their candidate. Nader was an attorney, author, and lecturer who had long been one of the most prominent environmental activists in the country. The Libertarian Party candidate was Harry Browne, a financial advisor and author from Tennessee.

During the general election, the candidates fielded questions about many topics, including domestic issues such as social security reform, tax reform, and healthcare, as well as numerous foreign policy issues. However, much of the campaign focused on personal attacks. Those supporting Gore criticized Bush's intelligence and lack of experience, while Bush's supporters claimed that Gore lacked the personality and charisma to lead a nation. Republicans also focused on the numerous scandals of the Clinton administration, attempting to imply that Gore was an extension of that legacy.

The presidential election occurred on Tuesday, November 7, 2000. As election results came in, it was apparent that the outcome would be close. Bush was successful in the South, as well as the central region of the country, while the states voting for Gore were in New England and on the West Coast.

Al Gore   *George W. Bush*

Early in the evening, major news outlets declared that Gore had won the state of Florida. This was a crucial victory for the Democratic candidate and all but assured his victory in the election. However, as the night wore on, the outcome in Florida grew uncertain. Reporters were forced to admit that they had called the state too early.

To win the presidency, a candidate must earn 270 votes in the Electoral College. Every state, except Florida, had been decided. Al Gore had 266 electoral votes, while George W. Bush had only 246. However, Florida's remaining 25 electoral votes would swing the election in favor of either candidate. Finally, at 2:30 AM (EST), Bush was declared the winner in Florida, also winning the presidency.

However, because the margin of victory in Florida was less than 2,000 votes, Gore was entitled to a recount. Following the recount process, this number had been reduced to just over 900 votes. Gore then asked for a manual recount of four counties. As the manual recount ensued, many irregularities were discovered, such as multiple candidates being voted for on the same ballot. Observers felt that some of these irregularities were being caused by the physical handling of the ballots, which was further skewing the results.

On November 26, Katherine Harris, the Florida Secretary of State, brought an end to the manual recount process, declaring George W. Bush the victor in Florida by a total of 537 votes. At that point, Al Gore filed a lawsuit, demanding that further recount results from Miami-Dade County and Palm Beach County be included. Gore lost this case, which he then appealed to the Florida State Supreme

Court. The Florida State Supreme Court ruled that a manual recount should be done in all counties, not just the four counties in question.

This decision was appealed to the United States Supreme Court by George W. Bush. Oral arguments for Bush v. Gore were heard by the US Supreme Court on December 11, 2000. The Supreme Court determined that individual ballots were being treated differently from precinct to precinct. Therefore, by a 7-2 vote, they ruled that this violated the Equal Protection Clause of the Fourteenth Amendment which states that all citizens will be granted equal protection of the laws. The Court also ruled, in a 5-4 vote, that the state of Florida uphold the December 12 deadline that had already been established for bringing this process to an end. These two decisions effectively ended the recount process, and George W. Bush was declared the winner in the state of Florida. This occurred well over one month after the actual election.

As a result, George W. Bush became the 43rd President of the United States. Despite his victory in the Electoral College, Bush actually received less popular votes than his opponent. Al Gore acquired 50,999,897 votes, while George W. Bush received 50,456,002. This was only the fourth time in US history that a candidate had won the Electoral College but lost the popular vote (the previous three times being the elections of 1824, 1876, and 1888).

One of the contributing factors that led to the final result in the 2000 election was the strong showing of third-party candidates. The Green Party candidate Ralph Nader accumulated more than 2.8 million votes, while Reform

Party candidate Pat Buchanan received more than 448,000. These totals may not seem high, but in an election decided by such a narrow margin of victory, small numbers of votes could have been critical in changing the outcome. For example, in the crucial state of Florida, Nader received 97,000 votes.

One other factor that many believe played a role in the election's outcome was the use of exit polling data to declare an early victory for Gore in Florida. Winning the state of Florida would have nearly ensured an Al Gore victory. This may have suppressed voter turnout in Western states where polls were still open. Many voters may have stayed home and not voted, believing the election was already decided. As a result of this election, news organizations and television networks have grown more cautious about declaring winners before all votes have been counted.

The presidential election of 2000 was one of the closest in American history. Its controversial outcome ensures that it will continue to be debated and studied for years to come.

George W. Bush

The 43rd President of the United States was George W. Bush. Who was George W. Bush? What happened during his presidency?

George Walker Bush was born in New Haven, Connecticut on July 6th, 1946. He was the first of what would eventually be six children born to George and Barbara Bush. He lived his young life in Midland, Texas and then Houston, Texas, but attended a boarding school in Massachusetts.

After graduating high school, Bush enrolled at Yale University in 1964. He graduated in 1968 with a degree in History. In 1973, he attended Harvard Business School, which he graduated from in 1975 with a Master's degree in Business Administration.

In 1977, Bush was introduced to Laura Welch, a librarian and school teacher. The two dated for three months and were married in November of that same year. George and

Laura would have two children together, Barbara and Jenna, twins who were born in 1981.

In 1977, Bush established a small company called Arbusto Energy. This company was involved in the exploration of oil and eventually changed its name to Bush Exploration. The company merged with a larger company, Spectrum 7, which Bush became the chairman of.

Bush's success in the oil industry allowed him to purchase the controlling interest of the Texas Rangers, a Major League Baseball team. Bush worked as the managing general partner for five years and played an active and visible role with the organization. Bush eventually sold his interest in the Rangers for $15 million.

In 1988, Bush's father, George HW Bush, ran for President of the United States. Bush worked closely with his father throughout the campaign, serving as a campaign adviser and speaking to the media. He also assisted his father during the 1992 presidential campaign when George HW Bush ran for reelection.

Bush announced that he would run for governor of Texas in 1994, opposing the Democratic incumbent, Anne Richards. Richards was a popular governor, and the two candidates battled each other in a heated campaign. Bush emerged victorious, winning 53.5% of the vote. Four years later, he was reelected with 69% of the vote, becoming the first governor in the history of Texas to be elected to two consecutive four-year terms.

As a popular governor of a large state, it was anticipated that he would run for president in 2000, which he did. He

George W. Bush

became the Republican nominee and competed against Democrat Al Gore for the presidency. The 2000 election is best remembered because of its incredibly close outcome. Gore received more popular votes, but Bush won the election in the Electoral College by the narrowest of margins. With his victory, George W. Bush became the 43rd President of the United States.

Bush's first term as president was dominated by foreign affairs. The terrorist attack on the World Trade Center in September of 2001 precipitated the larger "war on terror." Wars in both Afghanistan and Iraq resulted from the efforts to curtail terrorist activities.

Following the terrorist attack in 2001, Bush also signed the Patriot Act. This was a controversial measure that allowed government agencies to conduct surveillance on individuals with suspected terrorist ties. Additionally, the Bush administration created the Department of Homeland Security. This was a new cabinet-level department which became responsible for public security.

Domestically, Bush signed the "No Child Left Behind" Act. This was an education law which was designed to help narrow the gap between student performance in wealthy and underprivileged districts. The measure became controversial as critics felt it placed too much emphasis on standardized testing and was not properly funded.

Bush sought and won reelection in 2004. His opponent was John Kerry, a Democratic senator from the state of Massachusetts. Bush won 31 out of 50 states and 50.7% of the popular vote.

In Bush's second term, Hurricane Katrina devastated

coastal regions in Louisiana. It was one of the worst natural disasters in American history, causing more than $100 billion in damages. Many criticized President Bush for not doing enough to help those in need during the catastrophe.

Following his presidency, Bush retired from public life and attempted to maintain a low profile. He rarely made public appearances and did not typically express his political opinions or criticize his successors. He occasionally made public speaking appearances and took up painting as a hobby.

During his presidency, Bush was both one of the most popular and one of the most disliked presidents in history. Shortly after the terrorist attack on the World Trade Center in 2001, his approval ratings were well over 90%. However, later in his presidency, these numbers dipped as low as 19%. In the years since he left office, opinions of his overall job performance have varied. It may be years before the true impact of his presidency, whether positive or negative, is fully known or appreciated.

The September 11th Terrorist Attacks

The United States experienced a major terrorist attack on September 11th, 2001. What happened that day? What were the results of this attack?

The World Trade Center was a complex of seven structures in New York City. The most notable of these structures were the two buildings known as the "twin towers." These two structures each stood more than 1,300 feet and were amongst the tallest buildings ever con-structed. More than 50,000 people worked in the towers on a daily basis, and an additional 200,000 visited the World Trade Center on business-related matters or as tourists.

On February 26th, 1993, the World Trade Center became the target of a terrorist attack. A man named Ramzi Yousef placed a moving truck filled with 1,500 pounds of explosives in an underground parking garage. Six people perished from the blast that resulted, and an additional 1,042 were injured. This served as a precursor for the larger attack which would occur several years later.

On the morning of September 11th, 2001, four commercial airliners were hijacked by a group of nineteen terrorists. Five of these hijackers, onboard American Airlines Flight 11, crashed the plane into the North Tower of the World Trade Center at 8:46 AM. At 9:03 AM, a second plane, United Airlines Flight 175, was flown into the South Tower of the World Trade Center.

Just over thirty minutes later, at 9:37 AM, American Airlines Flight 77 was crashed into the Pentagon in Washington DC. A fourth flight, United Airlines Flight 93, was also hijacked. The hijackers intended to fly this plane into the Capitol Building in Washington DC. However, the passengers and crew attempted to recapture the plane from the hijackers. This struggle resulted in the plane crashing just southeast of Pittsburgh.

The damage, destruction, and ensuing fires in New York City resulted in the collapse of both World Trade Center towers. Additionally, debris from the enormous structures also caused one of the other five buildings in the World Trade Center complex to collapse. Damage at the Pentagon was also extensive, with a significant portion of the building being destroyed.

Emergency responders and other rescue personnel were immediately on each scene. Members of the New York City Police Department, the New York City Fire Department, and countless others worked tirelessly to rescue as many victims as possible. Additionally, police officers and firefighters from across the country volunteered their time and resources to join the rescue and recovery efforts. In Washington DC, rescue workers at the Pentagon included Secret Service agents and high ranking members of the military.

As rescue crews continued their work, investigators attempted to learn who was responsible for the heinous acts. It was eventually discovered that fifteen of the nineteen hijackers were Saudi Arabian, and the group was led by Mohamed Atta, an Egyptian. The group was a part of an extensive terrorist organization known as Al-Qaeda. The leader of Al-Qaeda was Osama bin Laden. Initially, bin Laden denied involvement, but he ultimately took responsibility for orchestrating the attacks. A second man, Khalid Sheikh Mohammed, also admitted to being heavily involved in the planning of the attack.

By the time the cleanup process was complete, 2,606 people had lost their lives in the attack on the World Trade Center. Another 125 individuals died at the Pentagon. Additionally, the 246 passengers and crew members aboard the four planes also perished. This means a total of 2,977 people lost their lives that day (this excludes the nineteen hijackers who also died).

The impact of the terrorist attacks on September 11th, 2001 was far-reaching and long-lasting. Americans became increasingly paranoid about the possibility of another attack. As a result, increased security measures at airports became commonplace. New pieces of legislation, such as the Patriot Act, allowed government officials to be more proactive with investigations of suspected terrorists. The Department of Homeland Security was also created to help better organize the various agencies responsible for US security. Also, the United States began to fight the "War on Terror" in various countries around the world, including Afghanistan.

The World Trade Center after the attack on September 11, 2001, with the Statue of Liberty in the foreground.

The War on Terror

In the early 2000s, the United States and many other countries began fighting the War on Terror. What was the War on Terror? How did it come to be?

Terrorism has been a major global issue for many decades. Countless political groups and religious organizations have used terrorist tactics in an effort to advance their causes. These tactics include taking hostages, bombings, hijacking airplanes, and other similar activities. Terrorist actions often result in a large number of deaths as well as the destruction of property.

For example, on October 23rd, 1983, a terrorist attack occurred in Beirut, Lebanon. Two bombs, planted inside large trucks, were detonated at a military barracks. The blasts killed 241 American soldiers as well as 58 French servicemen and six civilians. On December 21st, 1988, terrorists planted a bomb onboard Pan-Am Flight 103, resulting in the deaths of 270 people.

The most devastating terrorist attack in history occurred on September 11th, 2001. Terrorists hijacked four passenger planes and crashed them into the World Trade Center and the Pentagon. This attack resulted in the deaths of 2,977 individuals (excluding the nineteen terrorists who also died that day). In the aftermath of this horrendous act, several world leaders determined that the nations of the world could no longer remain idle and allow these attacks to continue.

In September of 2001, President George W. Bush first used the term "War on Terror" to describe the military and legal struggle that he believed should be fought against those who would commit such atrocities. President Bush stated that one of the primary goals of the War on Terror should be to identify and dismantle terrorist organizations, no matter where they existed. Some of the more notable terrorist groups throughout the 1980s and 1990s had included Hamas, Hezbollah, the Palestinian Liberation Organization (PLO), and the Irish Republican Army (IRA).

Bush also hoped to bring an end to state-sponsored terrorism. This meant that there were certain countries harboring terrorist and allowing them to establish camps and train within the borders of those nations. These countries were also supporting terrorist organizations financially and supplying them with weapons.

President Bush would eventually refer to these nations as the Axis of Evil. This was a group of rogue states thought to be harboring terrorist organizations. The countries listed as part of the Axis of Evil included Iraq, Iran, Syria, Libya,

Cuba, and North Korea. It was also thought that these nations could potentially be developing weapons of mass destruction, such as nuclear missiles or chemical weapons.

One of the first targets in the War on Terror was Al-Qaeda, the terrorist organization responsible for the September 11th attacks. It was discovered that Al-Qaeda primarily operated out of Afghanistan. Thus, in October of 2001, American and British forces invaded Afghanistan in a concentrated effort to destroy this organization and seek out Osama bin Laden (Al-Qaeda's leader).

In 2003, the War on Terror was taken to Iraq. Iraq had been a known supporter of state-sponsored terrorism since at least 1979. Additionally, it was thought that Iraq was attempting to develop weapons of mass destruction. Iraq's president, Saddam Hussein, was guilty of crimes against humanity and had committed many barbaric acts against his own people. In March of 2003, a coalition of countries, led by the United States, invaded Iraq and removed Saddam Hussein from power.

Another prominent terrorist organization targeted in the War on Terror was the Islamic State of Iraq and Syria, better known as ISIS (this group is also referred to as the Islamic State of Iraq and the Levant, or ISIL). ISIS has conducted many terrorist attacks throughout the world, resulting in much death and destruction. There have been numerous military actions carried out in an effort to curtail ISIS's activities. As of 2017, it was believed that ISIS had a presence in at least eighteen different countries.

The War on Terror had many critics. Some felt there was no way a war against terrorism could be fought since terrorism is a tactic rather than a definable enemy. Others believed the war was merely an excuse by governments to infringe on the civil liberties of their citizens. Still, others felt that conducting so many military campaigns at once, against a number of different enemies, was a drain on US military resources and a waste of financial resources.

In March of 2009, President Barack Obama requested that military officials no longer use the phrase "War on Terror." However, despite the fact that this phrase is no longer used officially, the objectives of bringing an end to state-sponsored terrorism continue. There is no doubt that acts of terrorism will remain a part of the world for years to come, and the United States and its allies will continue to combat these enemies whenever they arise.

President Barack Obama (second from left)
watches as US forces eliminate Osama bin Laden

The Afghanistan War

The United States invaded Afghanistan in 2001. What was the purpose of this invasion? What were the results?

Shortly after the terrorist attack on the World Trade Center on September 11th, 2001, the United States government discovered that the culprits were members of a terrorist organization known as Al-Qaeda. Al-Qaeda was a militant organization dedicated to practicing a funda-mentalist form of Islam. It was formed in the late 1980s by Osama bin Laden, who was still the leader of the group in 2001.

Al-Qaeda had been responsible for numerous terrorist attacks throughout the 1990s. For example, in 1992, Al-Qaeda detonated bombs at two different hotels in Yemen. The group attempted to assassinate President Bill Clinton in 1996 by planting a bomb on a bridge, but the attempt was thwarted by the Secret Service. In August of 1998, the US embassies in Tanzania and Kenya were bombed, resulting in the deaths of 224 people. Al-Qaeda also attacked the USS Cole, killing seventeen members of the US Navy and injuring thirty-nine more.

Al-Qaeda's primary bases of operation were located in Afghanistan. At their Afghani facilities, Al-Qaeda would recruit, indoctrinate, and train followers. It was estimated that anywhere from 10,000 to 20,000 young men had participated in activities at these camps prior to the World Trade Center attack in 2001. Additionally, the camps in Afghanistan were used as bases to import and distribute weapons as well as coordinate activities with other terrorist organizations.

A US soldier in Afghanistan

Al-Qaeda's presence in Afghanistan was made possible by the ruling body of Afghanistan, known as the Taliban. The Taliban is an organization that was founded in 1994 by Mullah Muhammed Omar. This group had taken control of Afghanistan in 1996 and enforced a strict interpretation of Sharia law (Islamic law).

The Taliban had committed many human rights abuses while in power in Afghanistan. They were guilty of numerous massacres, often killing hundreds of people at one time. They also withheld food to parts of the population, forcibly starving their own citizens. Additionally, the Taliban had burned crops, fields, and homes in some regions of the country. All of these things were done as part of an ethnic cleansing effort as the Taliban attempted to rid their nation of all non-Afghans. These actions resulted in the deaths of over 5,000 people, with more than 100,000 others being displaced from their homes.

When the United States invaded Afghanistan in 2001, the primary goals were to dismantle Al-Qaeda and remove the Taliban from power. By removing the Taliban from power, the US hoped to deny Al-Qaeda a safe base to operate from.

US military action in Afghanistan began on October 7th, 2001, and by November 12th, the Taliban had fled the capital city of Kabul. By December, they had also abandoned the city of Kandahar, which had been the Taliban's last remaining stronghold.

Members of Al-Qaeda and the Taliban fled into the Tora Bora Mountains where they occupied a network of underground bunkers and fortified caves. The United States used aerial bombardments and Special Forces units to eliminate these installations. These efforts lasted for more than a decade, with many members of Al-Qaeda and the Taliban disappearing into the mountainous terrain and never being captured.

Osama bin Laden evaded American forces until 2011. On May 2nd, 2011, he was shot and killed by US Navy SEALs. His death brought an end to a ten year long search for the man who had orchestrated the deadliest terrorist attack in the history of the world.

Osama bin Laden

Osama bin Laden was the mastermind behind the World Trade Center terrorist attack on September 11th, 2001. Who was Osama bin Laden? Why did he attack the United States?

Osama bin Laden was born on March 10th, 1957, in Riyadh, Saudi Arabia. His father was a successful business-man who had made billions of dollars in the construction industry. Osama was raised with three half-brothers and a half-sister.

In college, bin Laden studied business administration and economics, but he also had a strong interest in religion and spent time interpreting the Quran. He had been raised to be a devout Sunni Muslim and eventually adopted a very literal interpretation of Islam. Bin Laden believed that the Muslim world was facing a major turning point and that the only solution to their problems would be the complete transition to Sharia law.

In the late 1970s and 1980s, bin Laden fought alongside the Afghani freedom fighters, known as the Mujahideen, as they struggled to free Afghanistan from Soviet control. Through his family's wealth, bin Laden personally funded many of the Mujahideen camps and training facilities. Bin Laden became quite well-known throughout the Middle East for his role in this conflict. Eventually, as more Arabs became involved with the movement in Afghanistan, bin Laden created his own organization. Established in August of 1988, this new group would eventually be known as Al-Qaeda.

Throughout the early 1990s, bin Laden became increasingly critical of Saudi Arabia's ties to the United States. He disliked the US and viewed it as immoral. He also blamed American policies for many of the problems in the Middle East. Additionally, he believed that the US was controlled by Jews and that most of the world's problems were caused by Jewish actions. These outspoken views caused him to be exiled from Saudi Arabia but also drew many followers to his side.

Al-Qaeda became a prominent terrorist organization in the 1990s. The group assisted both militarily and financially with jihad (Islamic holy war, or struggle) which took place in Algeria, Egypt, and Afghanistan. Al-Qaeda was also believed to be linked to many terrorist attacks worldwide throughout the decade.

Osama bin Laden and Al-Qaeda declared war against the United States in August of 1996. Two years later, bin Laden issued a fatwa (an Islamic religious decree or opinion) declaring that every Muslim should consider it their duty to kill North Americans and their allies. On August 7th, 1998, Al-Qaeda perpetrated a major terrorist attack against the United States. Two separate truck-bombs were detonated simultaneously at the US embassies in Tanzania and Kenya. More than two hundred people were killed, and Osama bin Laden was placed on the Federal Bureau of Investigation's (FBI) Ten Most Wanted List. In 2000, Al-Qaeda also claimed responsibility for the bombing of the USS Cole off the coast of Yemen.

On September 11th, 2001, two airliners were hijacked and flown into the World Trade Center in New York City. A third airplane was hijacked and flown into the Pentagon. A fourth was also hijacked but crashed in Pennsylvania before reaching its intended target. In total, 2,996 individuals perished, and more than 6,000 were wounded in this attack. Osama bin Laden, and Al-Qaeda, eventually claimed responsibility for this incident. Bin Laden claimed that he had orchestrated the attack in retribution for the destruction caused by the United States and Israel during the Lebanon War in 1982.

Following the September 11th terrorist attack, the United States put a tremendous amount of effort and resources into finding and either capturing or killing Osama bin Laden. Military efforts in Afghanistan (where he was believed to be hiding) proved unsuccessful. The pursuit continued for nearly ten years but there was little credible information as to his whereabouts.

After almost a decade of searching, bin Laden was tracked down in Pakistan. On May 2, 2011, a team of US

NAVY SEALs infiltrated his compound with the intention of capturing him and bringing him to justice. During this operation, bin Laden was shot and killed. He was buried at sea the next day.

Osama bin Laden

The Patriot Act

In October of 2001, the Patriot Act was signed into law. What is the Patriot Act? What powers did it grant to the federal government?

In the aftermath of the terrorist attacks which occurred on September 11th, 2001, Americans were experiencing much anxiety. Many believed that the next terrorist attack could occur at any moment. In an effort to assuage these fears, and act proactively to prevent future attacks from happening, Congress passed the USA PATRIOT Act. President George W. Bush signed the new law on October 23rd, 2001.

USA PATRIOT is an acronym which stands for "Uniting and Strengthening America by Providing Appropriate Tools Required to Intercept and Obstruct Terrorism." The new law authorized government agencies to implement several different means for investigating suspected terrorists (which had not previously been available to them).

For example, one provision of the Patriot Act allowed government officials to view documents, and other information about suspects, without immediately notifying the individual that a warrant had been obtained for such documents. Another provision related to the placing of wiretaps on citizens' phones and other devices. The Patriot Act also made efforts to prevent money from being laundered in the United States and used to fund terrorism.

Other portions of the Patriot Act related to the Federal Bureau of Investigation (FBI), the Central Intelligence Agency (CIA), and the Department of Defense being able to demand data and records connected to certain individuals. This information could be asked for without probable cause, meaning that the agency in question would not have to prove that they had a reasonable suspicion that someone had committed a crime.

Bush signing the Patriot Act

The final provisions of the Patriot Act related to the definition of terrorism. Domestic terrorism was redefined to include a broader scope of activities, including assassination attempts, kidnapping, and mass destruction. Any activity which is dangerous to human life, violates the criminal laws of the United States, is intended to intimidate or coerce the population, or influence the policy of the government could be defined as terrorism.

The Patriot Act received heavy amounts of criticism. Many felt that politicians were taking advantage of a frightened populous in order to expand the government's ability to conduct surveillance on its own citizens. Proponents of civil liberties argued that many of the provisions in the Patriot Act were a violation of the 4th Amendment of the Bill of Rights, which protects citizens from "illegal search and seizure." Many aspects of the Patriot Act have been challenged in court with varied success.

The Patriot Act was reauthorized by both Presidents George W. Bush and Barack Obama. The Patriot Act officially expired in 2015 and was replaced by a modified and amended law known as the USA Freedom Act. There is little doubt that as long as terrorism is a topic in world affairs, the measures taken to monitor and surveil suspected terrorists will remain an issue.

The Department of Homeland Security

In 2001, a new cabinet-level department was created. What was this department called? What responsibilities does it have?

Following the terrorist attacks on September 11th, 2001, it was believed that the United States could do a more efficient job of coordinating the many agencies responsible for protecting its citizens. As a result, President George W. Bush announced the creation of a new cabinet-level position, the Office of Homeland Security. The next year, the Department of Homeland Security (DHS) was established, with Tom Ridge becoming the first Secretary of Homeland Security.

The Department of Homeland Security was intended to consolidate several existing government organizations into one. Ultimately, twenty-four different agencies would fall under the new department's jurisdiction. Each of these smaller agencies is responsible for some aspect of ensuring that Americans are secure within US borders. The organizations that the DHS is responsible for include the Federal Emergency Management Agency (FEMA), Immigration and Naturalization Services, US Customs, the US Coast Guard, the Secret Service, and many others.

Since its inception, the DHS has overseen many efforts in an attempt to protect the American people. For example, the department produced a series of public service announcements explaining the steps that should be taken in the event of a chemical attack. The DHS also encouraged families to devise a "family emergency plan" and create an emergency supply kit.

DHS also created the Homeland Security Advisory System. This was a color-coded scale that allowed the department to inform the American people of the existing "terrorist threat level." For example, if the level was "green," this meant the terrorist threat level was very low. Whereas, if the level was "red," it meant that the terrorist threat level was severe. The color-coated scale was replaced in 2011 with the National Terrorism Advisory System. This system was intended to more clearly communicate information to the citizens by releasing alerts and bulletins.

The Department of Homeland Security has received much scrutiny and criticism since its creation. The department is viewed by some as the ultimate example of excessive bureaucracy. It has often been the subject of reports and news articles related to government waste as investigators have uncovered that the agency has lost billions of dollars due to fraud and mismanaged funds.

It has also been accused of violating the civil liberties of many honest Americans who have not been implicated in any crimes. Searching luggage, opening mail, intercepting email and text messages, and listening to phone calls are just some of the activities conducted by various organizations under the DHS umbrella. Most of these incidents occurred in the name of protecting Americans from terrorism, but such acts have raised concerns amongst proponents of citizens' right to privacy.

Much of the negative criticism has been directed towards the Transportation Security Administration (TSA) which falls under the authority of the DHS. The TSA is primarily concerned with screening airline passengers at airports. TSA agents have been accused of abusing their authority by inappropriately searching individuals and even stealing from them. Many feel that the searches conducted by TSA officials are a violation of the 4th Amendment protection from illegal search and seizure.

In the modern world, the Department of Homeland Security is the third largest cabinet-level department. In 2017, more than 240,000 employees worked for DHS, a number which is likely to grow over time. The department's budget is more than $40 billion a year.

The Iraq War

In 2003, the United States invaded Iraq. Why did this invasion take place? What were the results of this event?

In the months leading up to the United States' invasion of Iraq, it was believed by high-ranking US government officials that Iraq was attempting to develop, or otherwise obtain, weapons of mass destruction. These weapons could have included chemical weapons such as sarin nerve gas, mustard gas, or even nuclear weapons. In fact, as far back as the Persian Gulf War in 1991, Iraq was known to have stockpiled uranium, which could be used in the manufacture of nuclear weapons.

It was also believed that Iraq's president, Saddam Hussein, was possibly supporting international terrorist organizations such as Al-Qaeda. Aside from Hussein's potential support of terrorism, he was also known to be a ruthless dictator who governed Iraq through fear and intimidation. He had been responsible for numerous atrocities within his own country and had caused the deaths of more than 200,000 Iraqi citizens.

Based on these reasons, President George W. Bush, and Prime Minister Tony Blair of the United Kingdom, determined that Hussein needed to be removed from power. In the spring of 2003, a coalition force made up of military personnel from the US, the UK, Australia, and Poland began preparing to make that happen. The stated goals of the military operation were to end the regime of Saddam Hussein, locate and eliminate Iraq's weapons of mass destruction, and capture or drive out any terrorists within that country.

The invasion of Iraq, led and orchestrated by General Tommy Franks, began on March 20th, 2003 and involved more than 300,000 troops from various countries. The initial attack was a simultaneous air and ground assault which came to be known as "shock and awe." This tactic was designed to overwhelm the opponent with an astounding display of force.

The rapid invasion demoralized the Iraqi soldiers. Many Iraqis abandoned their posts or willingly surrendered to the swiftly approaching US and British forces. The machinery and weapons being used by the Iraqi military were outdated and poorly maintained. As a result, there was initially very little resistance to the coalition onslaught.

After only three weeks, coalition troops had captured virtually every major city in Iraq, including the Iraqi capital of Baghdad. In early April of 2003, Saddam Hussein fled the city. The people of Iraq rejoiced, vandalizing posters and paintings with his image and tearing down statues which bore his likeness. Hussein was eventually tracked down and captured in December of 2003. He was placed on trial for crimes against humanity and was executed on December 30th, 2006.

On May 1, 2003, President Bush delivered a speech onboard the USS Abraham Lincoln in which he declared "mission accomplished" regarding the goals in Iraq. However, fighting continued for years following this speech. Forces who remained loyal to Saddam Hussein, or who opposed the US presence in Iraq, continued their resistance for the remainder of the decade. The United States would not officially withdraw all of its combat troops from Iraq until December of 2011.

The invasion of Iraq was a controversial decision at the time and remains so today. Many Americans, and others around the world, viewed this as an unprovoked act of aggression by the United States. There were large antiwar protests in many cities and countless outspoken critics of the actions of the Bush administration. Some argued that Bush was fighting the war to benefit his associates in the oil industry.

In 2007, polls showed that anywhere from 66% to 75% of the world's population disapproved of the US presence in Iraq. However, polls taken within Iraq illustrate that a majority of Iraqis were in favor of the US removing Hussein from power. Additionally, only about one-third of Iraqis were in favor of an immediate withdrawal of US troops.

There was also a heavy financial burden from the Iraq War. It has been estimated that the cost of the war efforts

Statue of Saddam Hussein being torn down

from 2003 to 2011 was approximately $1.7 trillion. There were other losses as well. More than 15,000 irreplaceable items were looted from the National Museum of Iraq.

Even more worrisome, however, is the fact that in the aftermath of the war, as much as 250,000 tons of explosives went missing. It is possible that many of these explosives ended up in the hands of individuals who could use them to commit further acts of terror.

There were many casualties in the Iraq War. There were 139 US soldiers killed, with another 551 wounded. Coalition forces suffered a combined loss of 172 soldiers. Iraqi deaths are much more difficult to calculate. There were many Iraqis who were left unaccounted for. Some fled the country, and the cause of death for many has been difficult to determine. Some organizations have put the number at 87,000, while others speculate that the death toll for Iraq could have exceeded one million people.

However, the Iraq War was not without its successes. Coalition forces did discover and destroy nearly 5,000 chemical weapons. Also, the people of Iraq were freed from the clutches of the ruthless dictator Saddam Hussein.

Saddam Hussein

The President of Iraq from 1979-2003 was Saddam Hussein. How did Saddam rise to power? What were the circumstances of his downfall?

Saddam Hussein was born on April 28th, 1937, a mere eight miles from Tikrit, Iraq. As a young man, he attended law school for three years but dropped out to join a revolutionary group known as the Ba'ath Party. The Ba'ath Party promoted pan-Arabism, a belief that the Arab world should unite as a single nation.

Saddam became a key figure in the Ba'ath Party, rapidly rising through the ranks of the organization. In 1958, he participated in an ill-fated attempt to assassinate Iraq's prime minister. Following the failed assassination attempt, Saddam escaped to Egypt where he lived until 1963. He returned to Iraq and was imprisoned in 1964. He remained in prison until 1967 when he managed to escape.

The next year, he participated in a coup which overthrew

the existing Iraqi government and resulted in Saddam becoming the vice president. As vice president, Saddam became highly influential in Iraqi society.

Saddam focused on bringing much-needed stability to the country. Iraq had long suffered from internal feuds between religious groups, such as the Sunni and Shia Muslims, and between ethnic groups like the Kurds and the Arabs. Saddam attempted to suppress these differences in the hopes of creating a more peaceful country. Saddam also modernized Iraq, promoting literacy programs, providing free public education, supplying electricity to nearly every city, and improving medical care.

In 1979, President Ahmed Hassan al-Bakr resigned after his health became extremely poor, and Saddam became president. Shortly after assuming power, Saddam held a meeting of Ba'ath Party leaders. At this meeting, he read a list of sixty-eight names who he believed had been "disloyal" to the party, and each of the men were removed from the room, one at a time. These individuals were placed on trial and found guilty of treason. Twenty-two of them were executed by a firing squad. Less than three weeks after Saddam had assumed the presidency, hundreds of Ba'ath Party officials had been executed.

While in power, Saddam used terror and intimidation to solidify his grip on Iraq. Countless individuals were tortured in gruesome fashion. The group which suffered the most was an ethnic group known as the Kurds. Saddam conducted a genocidal campaign with the intent of eliminating the Kurdish population in Iraq. It is estimated that somewhere between 50,000 to 100,000 Kurds died

Saddam Hussein

between 1986 and 1989, with some estimates rising as high as 182,000. Overall, approximately 250,000 Iraqis lost their lives due to Saddam Hussein's reign of terror.

As the country's leader, Saddam attempted to ensure that the people viewed him as a hero. Images of Saddam could be seen on posters, portraits, and in large murals on the sides of schools, shops, and office buildings. His image also appeared on Iraqi currency, and statues of Saddam could be found throughout Iraq. He also constructed a carefully crafted public image, frequently appearing in different outfits to please different segments of the population. For example, he would appear in business suits to project the image of a modern leader or he might dress in more traditional clothing to appease the nomadic Bedouins.

In 1991, Hussein narrowly escaped being removed from power by the United States after the Persian Gulf War. However, in 2003, a coalition of nations, led by the United States and the United Kingdom, determined that Hussein was a threat to international security. Coalition forces invaded Iraq, liberating the Iraqi people from Saddam's rule. Hussein evaded authorities until December of 2003 when he was captured by US military personnel. He was placed on trial for crimes against humanity and executed by hanging on December 30th, 2006.

Hurricane Katrina

One of the worst natural disasters in the history of the United States occurred in 2005. What happened? How did the nation cope with this event?

On August 23rd, 2005, a tropical storm developed over the Bahamas. The storm was named "Katrina" and was upgraded to a hurricane on August 25th as it approached land. As the hurricane made its way through the Gulf of Mexico, it became a "category 5" on August 28th. This is the strongest classification of hurricane, which can produce sustained winds of more than 157 miles per hour. Category 5 storms can cause significant structural damage to buildings and can uproot trees.

As the hurricane approached the mainland, it weakened to a category 3, but the US Coast Guard and the Federal Emergency Management Agency (FEMA) still began preparing the Southern coast of the United States for a potential disaster. Throughout the coastal regions of Louisiana, Mississippi, Alabama, and Florida, orders were given to evacuate. The mayor of New Orleans issued a mandatory evacuation for the first time in the city's history. Many citizens fled the region, while others hoped to ride out the storm in the safety of shelters provided by government agencies.

On August 29, 2005, torrential rain poured down as the storm surged onto land. Rainfall was between 8-10 inches, with some areas recording as much as 15 inches. As a result, the water levels in Lake Pontchartrain rose rapidly. The levees which held back the water were breached and massive flooding occurred in New Orleans.

Many places were subject to flooding throughout Louisiana, Mississippi, and Alabama, but New Orleans was particularly susceptible to flooding because the city sits below sea level. At one point, nearly 80% of New Orleans was submerged in water. More than 60,000 people became stranded by this flooding, with more than 33,500 of these being rescued by the US Coast Guard.

After the hurricane left the area, some residents who had remained behind began looting stores and businesses. Some searched for food and drinkable water, which was in short supply. Others stole televisions, stereos, sporting goods equipment, and anything else they could carry. There were also reports of car thefts, rapes, and even murders during the aftermath of the storm. More than 50,000 federal troops, national guardsmen, and local law enforcement officials were mobilized to restore order and aid with rescue and cleanup efforts.

More than one million people were displaced by Hurricane Katrina. FEMA provided thousands of mobile home trailers which were intended to be temporary housing for those who had been flooded out. FEMA also paid for more than 12,000 people to stay in hotel rooms while they attempted to reestablish themselves. Many who lost their homes never returned. The populations of Houston, Texas; Mobile, Alabama; and Baton Rouge, Louisiana all grew significantly, while the population of New Orleans decreased by more than 250,000 people.

This image shows fishing boats which have been left grounded by Hurricane Katrina.

There was significant ecological damage caused by Hurricane Katrina as well. It has been estimated that more than 200 square miles of land was permanently submerged in water. Much of this was coastal land that pelicans, turtles, ducks, and other animals had used for breeding. The habitats of many native birds and other wildlife was also disrupted. Forty-four oil production facilities were damaged during the storm, resulting in more than seven million gallons of oil spilling into the Gulf of Mexico. This further damaged the ecosystem for countless numbers of fish, turtles, and other sea life. Additionally, much of the floodwater from New Orleans was pumped back into Lake Pontchartrain. This water had been contaminated by bacteria, oil, chemicals, and raw sewage. This impacted the local fish populations within the lake.

In the weeks after the natural disaster occurred, countries from around the world displayed generosity towards the United States. Many contributed financially to help with relief efforts. For example, Kuwait donated $500 million, while the United Arab Emirates and Qatar each donated $100 million. Altogether, foreign governments contributed nearly $800 million. Other nations, such as India, Canada, Mexico, Germany, and Israel donated large quantities of blankets, beds, diapers, generators, and medical supplies.

The American people also displayed their generosity in the days following Hurricane Katrina. Organizations such as the Salvation Army and the American Red Cross accepted donations from across the US and around the world. Charitable organization collected a total of $4.25 billion from private individuals. The American Red Cross also provided 245,000 workers (most of whom were volunteers) to assist in the relief efforts.

Many people were critical of the government's reaction to Hurricane Katrina. Some felt that President George W. Bush and numerous federal agencies had not reacted quickly enough or provided adequate assistance to the areas devastated by the hurricane. Others felt that state and local officials had mismanaged the crisis.

The damage caused by Hurricane Katrina was nearly incalculable. Total property damage was estimated to be over $100 billion. Sadly, the hurricane also resulted in the deaths of 1,836 people. Two hundred and thirty-eight of these fatalities were in the state of Mississippi, while 1,577 people in the state of Louisiana lost their lives.

Daily Life and Popular Culture in the 2000s

The 2000s was a time of great change, and fully experiencing the decade meant embracing new technologies. What were some of these changes? How was life different than in previous decades?

In the 1990s, the American family began to look very different from the traditional model of a father, mother, and two children. This trend continued in the 2000s, as more and more single-parent families emerged. Also, as parents divorced and remarried, many children found themselves with parents and step-parents.

Young adults began delaying marriage until later in life. In 2000, 31% of women between the ages 20-24 were already married. By 2010, only 19% of women in the same age demographic were married. Also, many young adults began choosing to stay at home and delay "living on their own" until later in life. By the end of the decade, approximately 30% of young American adults between the ages of 18-34 were still living with their parents.

The decision for young adults to remain at home was due, in part, to the turbulent financial climate of the 2000s. Both income and housing prices fluctuated throughout the decade. For example, in 2000, the average income was $42,350, but by the end of the decade, the average income was only about $39,400. Meanwhile, the price of a new home in 2000 was $136,150, yet, by 2007, this amount had skyrocketed to $313,600. By 2010, the price of a new home had lowered slightly to $272,900.

The prices of other items were also inconsistent. In 2000, the price of a gallon of gasoline was $1.26. By 2008, gas prices had reached $3.39 a gallon, but by 2010, the price had once again fallen to $2.73. The prices of automobiles were slightly more stable throughout the decade. A new car cost $24,750 at the beginning of the decade and averaged about $27,950 by 2010. Of course, the prices of all items would have varied based on brand name, make, model, and region of the country.

The Internet revolutionized American lives in the 2000s. Most Americans had received their first glimpse of the Internet in the 1990s, but it was in the 2000s when the true impact of the new technology began to be understood. Average American families began shopping online, listening to music online, watching television shows and movies online, and even meeting potential dating partners online.

Electronic mail, or E-mail, made written communication instantaneous, and social networking websites allowed people to remain connected and experience the lives of "friends" like never before. Regardless of what one was interested in, they could now connect with thousands of others who shared similar interests, whether it be independent films, online gaming, fan fiction, or a local band.

The cell phone also had a significant impact on American lives. While "mobile phones" had been in existence since the early 1980s, the devices did not become practical and affordable until the late 1990s. Throughout the decade of the 2000s, they became increasingly commonplace. In 2000, just under 30% of Americans had a cell phone, but by 2010, approximately 85% of Americans owned one.

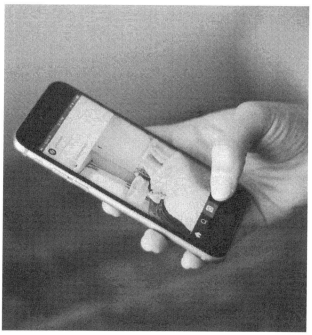

Cell phones became increasingly common throughout the 2000s.

In other areas of the life, some American families started to become more health conscious. Counting calories and checking the ingredients in food products became increasingly common. As a result, many American consumers began buying organic groceries. This meant attempting to purchase food that had been produced more naturally, without the use of pesticides, chemical fertilizers, or genetic engineering.

Some Americans also became more environmentally-conscious during the 2000s. Many cities enacted recycling programs and schools placed more emphasis on environmental concerns. From driving a more fuel-efficient vehicle to purchasing environmentally friendly light bulbs and reusable shopping bags, many Americans began making increased efforts to protect the environment.

Americans have always loved to travel, and the 2000s were no exception. However, following the terrorist attacks on September 11th, 2001, airline travel in America became increasingly difficult. New security measures required passengers to pass through metal detectors, have bags searched, and be patted down by security officials before entering airports and airplanes. This had a significant impact on Americans, since travelers now had to arrive at airports hours before flights and family members could no longer greet weary travelers directly off of the airplane.

Despite the emergence of the Internet, television remained the dominant form of entertainment in the 2000s. The most popular program of the decade was *American Idol*, a singing competition in which amateur performers were judged by celebrities. *American Idol* assumed the top spot in the ratings in 2005 and remained there for the rest of the decade. Another competition-based program, *Dancing With the Stars*, also proved very popular throughout the latter half of the decade.

Reality television became one of the staples of American TV throughout the 2000s. Originally made popular by MTV's *The Real World* in the 1990s, many other programs mimicked the show's style in the 2000s. *Big Brother*, *Survivor*, and *The Bachelor* were amongst the most popular reality TV series.

More traditional programs remained popular as well. *CSI: Crime Scene Investigation*, *Lost*, *Grey's Anatomy*, and *Desperate Housewives* were amongst the most popular hour-long dramas. *Everybody Loves Raymond*, *Will & Grace*, and *Two and a Half Men* were amongst the most popular sitcoms.

At the theater, American audiences fell in love with superheroes. *Batman Begins*, *Spiderman*, and *Iron Man* were just a few of the comic book themed movies that people flocked to see. *The Lord of the Rings* trilogy proved to be a huge box office success while garnering seventeen Academy Awards. Animated films such as *Monsters Inc.*, *Finding Nemo*, and *The Incredibles* entertained young audiences.

Americans continued their love affair with professional sports in the 2000s. The National Football League (NFL) produced many outstanding players during the decade. Tom Brady and the New England Patriots played in four Super Bowls, winning three championships. Peyton Manning was named the league MVP four times throughout the decade (an award he won five times during his career).

Kobe Bryant was the dominant player in the National Basketball Association. Bryant won four NBA championships and was selected to the All-Star team each year of the decade. Lebron James, Shaquille O'Neal, Tim Duncan, and Kevin Garnett were also phenomenal players.

Albert Pujols took Major League Baseball by storm, hitting 37 home runs in his first season and winning the National League Rookie of the Year award in 2001. Pujols would go on to be a nine time all-star and hit more than 600 home runs. Ichiro Suzuki became the first Japanese position player to excel in Major League Baseball. Ichiro played in ten MLB All-Star games and won ten Gold Glove awards throughout the rest of the decade. Alex Rodriguez and Barry Bonds were also dominant players during the era. However, their careers were marred by accusations of using performance-enhancing drugs, such as steroids or human growth hormones.

In music, the most successful artists at the beginning of the decade were pop stars such as Britney Spears and Christina Aguilera. Eminem and Usher also had sustained success throughout the decade. Groups such as Fallout Boy and Blink-182 were popular. In country music, American Idol winner Carrie Underwood became a sensation, while Toby Keith and Kenny Chesney continued successful careers that began in the 1990s.

It should be remembered that not everyone experienced the 2000s in the same way. These were just a few of the broad trends that were predominant throughout the decade. Each family and each individual had a unique situation, with their own stories, tastes, and preferences.

Steve Jobs and Apple

One of the most influential people in the modern era was Steve Jobs. What company did Jobs found? How did Jobs shape the modern world?

Steve Jobs was born in San Francisco, California on February 24th, 1955. He was immediately given up for adoption and raised by his adoptive parents, Paul and Clara Jobs. Steve had a difficult childhood as he was socially awkward and often bullied. He misbehaved at school and had a tendency to resist authority figures.

He became interested in electronics at a young age. By the age of thirteen, he was working for Hewlett-Packard, helping assemble frequency counters. After graduating high school, he briefly attended Reed College in Portland, Oregon. However, he dropped out because his parents could not afford it. After leaving college, Jobs picked up glass soda bottles for money, slept on the floor in friends' dorm rooms, and even received free meals from charitable organizations.

In 1976, a friend named Steve Wozniak showed Jobs a computer he had constructed. Jobs suggested that the two men sell such computers, which eventually became known as the Apple I. Together, Jobs and Wozniak formed Apple Computers and operated the business out of Jobs' garage.

In 1977, Apple introduced the Apple II, which became the company's first highly successful consumer product. Over the next several years, Apple continued to experience success. Jobs became a millionaire at the age of twenty-three. A year later, he was worth $10 million, and by the time he was twenty-five, he was worth $100 million.

Apple continued to revolutionize the home computer market throughout the early 1980s. In 1983, the company released the Apple Lisa, which Time magazine referred to as the "Machine of the Year." The next year, Apple introduced the Macintosh, which became one of the first mass-marketed personal computers to reach a large number of homes.

Jobs left Apple Inc. in 1985 and pursued other lucrative business ventures. However, he returned to the company in 1997 and was eventually named the Chief Executive Officer (CEO). He maintained his position as Apple's CEO until his death in 2011.

Throughout the late 1990s and 2000s, Apple introduced many new and innovative products which helped to shape the modern world. The iMac, the iPod, iTunes, the iPhone, and the iPad have become a part of the average American's everyday life.

Many of these devices achieved commonplace status

virtually overnight. For example, the iPad was introduced to the public in 2010, and by 2015, more than 250 million had been sold. Likewise, the iPhone, released in 2007, had sold more than one billion units by 2016.

Steve Jobs was diagnosed with pancreatic cancer in 2003. He passed away in October of 2011 due to complications related to this condition. Jobs almost certainly solidified his place in history, and his impact on society will be felt for decades to come.

Steve Jobs

The 2008 Presidential Election

The presidential election of 2008 was a historic occurrence. Who was involved in this election? What made it so significant?

The 2008 presidential election offered a wide variety of candidates who vied for the nation's top position. On the Republican side, President George W. Bush had served his full two terms and therefore was not eligible for re-election. His vice president Dick Cheney chose not to seek the presidency himself. This left the Republican field wide open.

A host of candidates sought the Republican nomination, including the former governor of Arkansas, Mike Huckabee, the former governor of Massachusetts, Mitt Romney, Representative Ron Paul of Texas, and the former Mayor of New York City, Rudy Giuliani. However, it was Senator

John McCain of Arizona who prevailed in the Republican primaries. McCain received his stiffest competition from Romney and Huckabee but secured his party's nomination by the end of March.

In the Democratic Party, the primary challengers were Senator Barack Obama of Illinois, Senator Hillary Clinton of New York, and John Edwards, a former senator from North Carolina. The former governor of New Mexico, Bill Richardson, and Representative Dennis Kucinich of Ohio also campaigned early in the race. Obama and Clinton battled each other through a long, hard-fought primary season, and Obama eventually prevailed in early June.

At their respective party conventions, Barack Obama officially accepted the Democratic nomination on August 28th, 2008, choosing Senator Joe Biden of Delaware as his vice presidential running mate. Barack Obama became the first African American to represent one of the two main political parties as a presidential nominee. Meanwhile, John McCain accepted the Republican nomination on September 4th, 2008, selecting Sarah Palin, the governor of Alaska, as his vice presidential running mate.

During the campaign, McCain argued that he was the more experienced of the two candidates. He had served in the United States Senate for more than twenty years and had also served in the United States Navy. Whereas, his opponent had only been in the US Senate for four years and had no military experience.

Obama responded by suggesting that McCain was too old for the position. At the age of 72, McCain would have been the oldest person ever elected president. Obama appealed to younger voters by implying that McCain's principles were outdated, or old-fashioned. He stressed a theme of "hope" and "change." Obama suggested that after eight years of Republican leadership, it was time for a different direction.

Obama's message resonated with American voters. When the election occurred on November 4th, 2008, Obama won convincingly, garnering 52.9% of the popular vote to McCain's 45.6%. In the Electoral College, Obama received 365 votes to McCain's 173 (270 votes were needed to win).

With his victory, Barack Obama became the 44th President of the United States. He also became the first African American to hold the highest office in the land.

Barack Obama   *John McCain*

Barack Obama

In 2008, Barack Obama became the first African American President of the United States. What did Barack Obama do before he became president? How did he achieve that position?

Barack Hussein Obama was born in Honolulu, Hawaii on August 4th, 1961. His father was from Kenya while his mother was a white woman from Wichita, Kansas.

After high school, Obama attended Occidental College in Los Angeles, starting in 1979. Two years later, he transferred to Columbia University in New York City. He graduated from Columbia in 1983 with a degree in political science. He worked for a brief time with the Business International Corporation and the New York Public Interest Research Group.

In 1985, Obama was hired as the director of the

Developing Communities Project. In this role, he helped establish a college preparatory tutoring program, a jobs training program, and a tenants' rights organization.

In 1988, Obama enrolled at Harvard Law School where he served as the editor for the Harvard Law Review. The next year, he became the president of that journal, the first African American to hold this position. After graduating from Harvard in 1991, he signed a publishing contract for a book which would eventually be titled Dreams from My Father, which was published in 1995.

Obama was hired to teach constitutional law at the University of Chicago Law School. He held this position for twelve years, from 1992 to 2004. During that time, he also directed Project Vote, a voter registration campaign which succeeded in registering more than 150,000 African Americans to vote.

In 1996, Obama was elected to the Illinois Senate. He was re-elected in both 1998 and 2002 (in 2000 he left the seat in an unsuccessful bid for a seat in the US House of Representatives). In 2004, Obama delivered the keynote address at the 2004 Democratic National Convention. This speech was well-received and propelled Obama onto the national stage. That same year he was elected to the United States Senate, winning 70% of the vote.

In February of 2007, Barack Obama announced his candidacy for President of the United States. He won a hard-fought primary election against former First Lady Hillary Clinton to become the Democrat nominee. In the general election, he was matched against the Republican candidate, John McCain. He defeated McCain, winning 365

Barack Obama as a senator in 2005

electoral votes to McCain's 173. He also won 52.9% of the popular vote. With this election, Obama became the first African American elected president.

In 2009, Obama was awarded the Nobel Peace Prize for his "extraordinary efforts to strengthen international diplomacy and cooperation between peoples". He was only the fourth American president to win the award.

Obama was re-elected to the presidency in 2012, once again winning by a sizeable majority. In the 2012 election, he received 51.1% of the popular vote, making him the first Democrat since Franklin Roosevelt to win a majority of the popular vote in two elections.

The Obama Administration

During Barack Obama's two terms as president, his administration had many accomplishments, as well as a few setbacks. What were some of the significant accomplishments? What were the setbacks?

The most significant reform of Barack Obama's first term was an attempt to overhaul America's healthcare system. The Democratic Party had long attempted to reform the nation's healthcare system, and after taking office, Obama made the issue a top priority. He and other Democrats believed that too many Americans lacked health insurance. Obama hoped to create a new system that would allow more Americans to be insured while also attempting to lower healthcare costs.

Multiple versions of healthcare legislation passed through the House of Representatives and the Senate. After considerable debate, both houses of Congress agreed on the same version of a bill. Officially titled the Patient Protection and Affordable Care Act, the bill eventually became known as the Affordable Care Act (ACA). Due to the president's involvement with the passage of the legislation, supporters and critics both began referring to the new healthcare bill as "Obamacare."

The Affordable Care Act established an individual mandate for health insurance. This means that every individual was required to have some form of health insurance, or otherwise pay a fine. The measure also established health insurance exchanges. These were online marketplaces where small businesses and individuals could purchase insurance from private companies. The ACA also placed restrictions on denying an individual a health insurance policy based on a pre-existing condition. These were just a few of the provisions laid out in the more than 20,000 pages of regulations associated with the law. Supporters praised the Affordable Care Act for helping many Americans gain health insurance. In 2010, the year of the ACA's passage, approximately 20% of the population was uninsured. By 2015, this number had dropped to just over 13%. However, the program was criticized by many. Opponents saw the program as an unnecessary enlargement of the federal government, and in some cases, it actually raised the cost of health insurance.

Education also became an emphasis during Obama's first term. One hundred billion dollars was set aside to supplement the budgets of public schools, fund special education, and assist low-income students. As part of this effort, President Obama and his Secretary of Education, Arne Duncan, introduced the Race to the Top program in July of 2009. This measure encouraged states to adopt a system of common curriculum standards. These standards became known as the Common Core State Standards Initiative (or Common Core) and were eventually adopted by 42 states. Proponents praised the standards for emphasizing language arts, reading skills, and mathematics. Meanwhile, critics argued that education was not a function of the federal government and that curriculum should be left up to the individual states.

In 2010, the Deepwater Horizon offshore oil drilling rig, just off the coast of Louisiana and Mississippi, experienced an explosion. The incident resulted in more than 4.9 million barrels of oil spilling into the Gulf of Mexico. This became the world's largest accidental oil spill and covered more than 68,000 square miles of water. In response, President Obama extended a ban on offshore oil drilling in May of 2010.

Another major issue of Obama's first four years in office was immigration reform. In 2010, the president supported a piece of legislation known as the Development, Relief, and Education of Alien Minors Act (DREAM Act). This bill would have granted permanent residency to immigrant minors who met certain qualifications. However, the legislation failed to pass Congress. In 2012, President Obama bypassed Congress and signed an executive order known as Deferred Action for Childhood Arrivals (DACA). This policy protected undocumented immigrants who had been brought to the United States prior to the age of sixteen.

Deportation would be deferred for two years, with the possibility of renewing the deferment every two years. DACA would eventually protect about 700,000 un-documented immigrants from deportation.

A harrowing chapter in American history came to a close during Obama's first term. Since the terrorist attack on September 11, 2001, the United States had been searching for Osama bin Laden, the leader of Al-Qaeda (the terrorist organization responsible for the attack). In the spring of 2011, bin Laden was tracked to a compound in Pakistan. As Commander-in-Chief of United States Armed Forces, President Obama authorized a strike by US Navy SEALs. On May 1, 2011, the SEALs conducted this raid, which resulted in bin Laden's death.

In 2012, President Obama ran for re-election. His opponent was Republican Mitt Romney (a former governor of Massachusetts). Obama won 51.1% of the popular vote and garnered 332 electoral votes to Romney's 206. The victory allowed Obama to tackle new issues in his second term.

Environmental concerns became a priority in 2013. Obama signed an executive order instructing the Environ-mental Protection Agency (EPA) to institute stricter carbon emission limits. Also, in 2015, a proposal known as the Clean Power Plan was unveiled. The goal of this plan was to reduce greenhouse gas emissions in the US by 26-28% by the year 2025.

Additionally, the president opposed the construction of the Keystone XL Pipeline. This pipeline would have been more than 1,000 miles long and connected oil fields in

Canada with the Gulf of Mexico. Those who opposed the pipeline argued that it would have contributed to global warming and to the nation's continued dependency on fossil fuels. Those who supported the pipeline pointed to the economic benefits that would have resulted from the pipeline's existence. In February of 2015, Obama vetoed a bill which would have authorized the pipeline's construction.

In foreign policy, activities in the Middle East and North Africa dominated both of Obama's terms. In 2011, a string of protests and uprisings throughout the Arab world became known as the Arab Spring. Tunisia, Egypt, Syria, and Libya were amongst the countries affected by this unrest. The Egyptian president, Hosni Mubarak, was forced to resign amidst the turmoil. Anti-government protests also took place in Syria, which eventually devolved into civil war. In 2014, a terrorist organization known as the Islamic State of Iraq and Syria (ISIS) emerged from this fighting. ISIS proved to be a formidable threat throughout Obama's second term. The Obama administration used airstrikes and other military actions to combat this new menace.

The Obama administration was no stranger to scandal and criticism. Several significant scandals plagued the presidency throughout its eight years. Most notably, on September 11, 2012, the American diplomatic compound in Benghazi, Libya was attacked, resulting in the deaths of two Americans. Several hours later, a second attack on a different facility caused two more deaths. Obama's Secretary of State, Hillary Clinton, received much criticism for not providing enough security at the installations.

Another scandal involved the Bureau of Alcohol, Tobacco, and Firearms (ATF). In an effort to track guns sold illegally to drug cartel leaders, the agency allowed licensed firearms dealers to sell weapons to illegal buyers. After these guns were used in crimes, the ATF came under heavy criticism. Obama's Attorney General, Eric Holder, was held in contempt of Congress for refusing to disclose documents related to the case. Both he and President Obama maintained that they were largely unaware of the operation until after it had concluded. This incident, and the investigation surrounding it, became known as the "Fast and Furious" scandal.

Barack Obama served eight years as president. He was the country's first African American Chief-of-State and had many accomplishments to speak of. As more time passes, history will gain a better understanding of his impact on the United States.

The Obamas meeting with Pope Benedict XVI

Michelle Obama

In 2009, Michelle Obama became First Lady of the United States. What did Michelle Obama do before she became First Lady? What are her accomplishments?

Michelle Obama was born as Michelle Robinson in Chicago, Illinois on January 17, 1964. Her father, Fraser Robinson, worked in the city water plant, while her mother, Marian, was a homemaker. She has one older brother named Craig.

As a child, Michelle was a good student who learned how to play the piano. She attended church regularly and took advanced courses in high school. Michelle graduated as the salutatorian of her class in 1981. She was accepted to Princeton University where she majored in sociology. She graduated from Princeton in 1985 and went on to attend Harvard Law School.

After completing law school, Michelle joined the law firm Sidley & Austin. While working with this law firm, she met Barack Obama. The two became close and married in October of 1992. The couple would go on to have two daughters, Malia and Sasha.

Aside from her work as a lawyer, Michelle Obama also held several other positions throughout the 1990s. She worked for the City of Chicago as an assistant to the mayor and as Assistant Commissioner of Planning and Development. She also served as the Executive Director for the Chicago office of a non-profit organization known as Public Allies (an organization that encouraged kids to focus on social issues).

Obama served as the Associate Dean of Student Services for the University of Chicago in 1996. In 2002, she became the Executive Director of Community Affairs for the University of Chicago Hospitals before becoming the Vice President for Community and External Affairs.

After Barack Obama's election to the presidency, Michelle became First Lady of the United States. As First Lady, she attempted to bring attention to numerous issues. She became a strong advocate of military families, promoted the arts and art education, and visited homeless shelters. Obama's most significant initiative came in 2010 when she announced the *Let's Move!* campaign. This was a far-reaching program intended to tackle the growing problem of childhood obesity. The stated goals of the plan included creating a healthy start for children, providing healthy food in schools, improving access to healthy foods, and increasing physical activity.

Let's Move! introduced new guidelines for nutritional information on food packaging, as well as recommendations from the United States Department of Agriculture (USDA) regarding school lunches. This included suggestions related to nutritional food choices and recommendations concerning serving sizes.

Obama has also authored two books, American Grown and Becoming. Since leaving the White House, she has remained busy, speaking at various engagements and continuing to advocate for numerous causes.

Michelle Obama, America's first African American First Lady, will always be remembered for her grace, elegance, and style. As all First Ladies have, she placed a unique stamp on the position and will almost certainly serve as a role model for future First Ladies, as well as for young women, for years to come.

The Obama family in 2011

The 2016 Presidential Election

In the year 2016, Donald Trump and Hillary Clinton faced off in a historic presidential election. Who won this strenuous contest? What was the campaign between these two like?

As the year 2016 approached, President Barack Obama was completing his second term. According to the Twenty-second Amendment, a president is only allowed to be elected to two terms. This meant he was ineligible to run for a third term, and new candidates would be seeking the office.

On the Republican side, many qualified candidates vied for the nomination, including Senator Ted Cruz of Texas, Senator Marco Rubio of Florida, Senator Rand Paul of Kentucky, and businesswoman Carly Fiorina of California. A number of governors also sought to become the Republican nominee including Rick Perry of Texas, Scott

Walker from Wisconsin, Jeb Bush from Florida, Bobby Jindal of Louisiana, and John Kasich of Ohio. However, it was real estate mogul and popular television personality Donald J. Trump that captured the nation's attention. Trump's strongest opposition came from Senator Cruz who won primaries in Texas, Oklahoma, Kansas and several other states. However, Trump eventually pulled away to become the Republican candidate. Trump selected Mike Pence, Governor of Indiana, as his vice presidential running mate, and the two formally accepted the Republican nomination on July 21, 2016 at the Republican National Convention in Cleveland, Ohio.

The early favorite to win the Democratic nomination was Hillary Clinton. Clinton had served as Secretary of State during the Obama Administration, and had also been elected as a senator from New York. She had also previously spent time in the White House, serving as First Lady during the presidency of her husband, Bill Clinton. Her only significant challenger in the Democratic Primaries was Bernie Sanders, a senator from Vermont. Sanders managed to win primary election in twenty-three states, but Clinton eventually prevailed. She chose Tim Kaine, a senator from Virginia, as her vice presidential running mate, and they formally accepted the Democratic nomination at the Democratic National Convention on July 28, 2016 in Philadelphia, Pennsylvania. Clinton became the first woman to represent one of America's two major parties as a presidential nominee.

During the general election, Clinton focused on expanding women's rights, making improvements to the

Affordable Care Act (healthcare), tax reform, and providing a path to citizenship for illegal immigrants.

Trump's campaign used the slogan "Make America Great Again," and emphasized protecting and reinforcing America's borders. He portrayed himself as a political outsider, who could clean up Washington D.C. by "draining the swamp."

The campaign was marred by scandal and personal attacks on both sides. Throughout the campaign, Clinton faced allegations that she had inappropriately used a private email address during her time as Secretary of State. Questions related to this FBI investigation persisted throughout the summer and into the fall. Her opponents questioned her ethical integrity, and also reminded voters of the many scandals associated with her husband's presidency. Additionally, Clinton insulted many potential voters by referring to Trump's supporters as "a basket of deplorables" who she believed were racist, sexist, xeno-phobic, and Islamaphobic.

Meanwhile, Trump's moral character was brought into question. In October of 2016, a video was released which showed Trump, in 2005, making lurid and obscene remarks about women. The video sparked outrage from opponents and supporters alike. Many Republican leaders even called on the nominee to step down and allow someone else to take his place. However, Trump refused to step aside. He apologized for the remarks made in the video, and pressed on with his campaign.

The negative issues faced by both candidates throughout the campaign led many people to consider third party options. Many Republicans who disliked Donald Trump began to consider voting for the Libertarian Party candidate Gary Richardson, former governor of New Mexico. Richardson also became an option for Democrats who had supported Bernie Sanders. Many Sanders supporters also turned to Green Party candidate Jill Stein. Stein was a doctor who had worked as an environmental activist for many years prior to her nomination.

The presidential election occurred on Tuesday, November 8, 2016. As election results came in, it was apparent that the outcome would be close. Trump was successful in the South, as well as the central region of the country, while the states voting for Clinton were in New England and on the West Coast. The difference in the election proved to be Midwestern states such as Michigan, Ohio, and Pennsylvania. These were all states that had voted Democratic in 2012, but voted Republican in 2016.

Hillary Clinton   *Donald Trump*

Hillary Clinton received 65.8 million votes. This was more than Donald Trump, who received 62.9 million votes. However, to win the presidency, a candidate must earn 270 votes in the Electoral College. Despite her vote total, Clinton won only twenty states, garnering 227 electoral votes. Meanwhile, Trump won thirty states, collecting 304 electoral votes. With his victory in the Electoral College, Donald Trump became the 45th President of the United States. This election was only the fifth time in American history that the winner of the Electoral College did not also win the popular vote (this also happened in the elections of 1824, 1876, 1888, and 2000).

The presidential election of 2016 was one of the most contentious in American history. Its controversial outcome ensures that it will continue to be debated and studied for years to come.

Hillary Rodham Clinton

The Democrat nominee for president is Hillary Clinton. Who is Hillary Clinton? What are some of her major accomplishments?

Hillary Rodham was born on October 26th, 1947, in Chicago, Illinois. At the age of three, her family moved to a Chicago suburb, Park Ridge, where she lived throughout her young life. She attended public school and participated in the Girl Scouts. During high school, she wrote for the school newspaper and was active in her school's student council.

After graduating high school, she enrolled at Wellesley College, a private women's college in Wellesley, Massachusetts. She majored in political science and graduated with a bachelor's degree in 1969. She became the first woman to speak at a Wellesley College commencement ceremony and received a standing ovation for her efforts. After graduating from Wellesley, she attended Yale Law

School, which she graduated from in 1973 with a law degree.

While attending Yale, she met Bill Clinton. The two dated for several years and eventually moved to Arkansas, where they were married in 1975. Hillary joined the prestigious Rose Law Firm in 1977, and in 1979, became its first female full partner. Meanwhile, Bill was elected Governor of Arkansas in 1978. Bill Clinton served as governor for eleven of the next thirteen years (he was defeated for reelection in 1980, but won again in 1982).

As First Lady of Arkansas, Clinton continued her practice as a lawyer, but was also appointed chairperson of the Rural Health Advisory Committee. Throughout her legal career, she was a strong advocate of children's rights. She served on the board of directors for the Arkansas Children's Hospital Legal Services and the Children's Defense Fund. Additionally, she served on the board of directors for TCBY (a yogurt company), LaFarge (an industrial company that specializes in concrete), and Wal-Mart.

During her time as First Lady of Arkansas, she also gave birth to her and Bill's only child, Chelsea. She was named Arkansas Woman of the Year in 1983 and Arkansas Mother of the Year in 1984. She also worked to establish mandatory teacher testing for the state, as well as creating statewide education curriculum standards and placing limits on classroom sizes.

In 1992, Bill Clinton announced he was running for president, and, as a result, Hillary Clinton received national attention for the first time. Throughout his campaign, Bill assured the nation that they would be getting "two for the price of one" and openly acknowledged that Hillary would play a significant role in his administration.

Hillary Clinton became First Lady of the United States in 1993, after Bill won the presidency. During her years as First Lady, she became more actively involved in her husband's administration than any First Lady since Eleanor Roosevelt. She was also the first First Lady to have an office in the West Wing of the White House (which is usually reserved for the president and the president's immediate staff).

She was appointed to head up the Task Force on National Healthcare Reform and also helped to create the Office on Violence Against Women at the Department of Justice. She also initiated the Adoption and Safe Families Act, a piece of legislation which corrected problems with the foster care system. This bill was passed by Congress, and signed into law by President Clinton, in 1997.

In 2000, as the Clintons were preparing to leave the White House, Hillary Clinton announced her intention to run for a seat in the United States Senate in New York. She won this election and was reelected to the Senate in 2006. During her time in the Senate, she served on five different Senate committees, including the Armed Services Committee and the Budget Committee.

Senator Clinton announced that she was running for president in 2008. During the 2008 Democratic primaries, she won twenty-three states, including victories in California, New York, Florida, Texas, and Ohio. However, she eventually lost the nomination to Barack Obama, who went on to win the general election as well.

After his election, Obama announced that Hillary Clinton

Hillary Clinton as a senator in 2005

was his first choice to become Secretary of State. She accepted this position and was sworn in as the Secretary of State on January 21, 2009. She became the first former First Lady to serve in a Cabinet level position.

During her time as Secretary of State, Clinton visited 112 countries, more than any other Secretary of State in history. While she was Secretary of State, she worked to build relationships with foreign nations and dealt with problematic situations in places such as Afghanistan, Egypt, and Libya, amongst many others. Following President Obama's reelection to the presidency in 2012, Clinton announced her resignation as Secretary of State, stating that she was not interested in a second term in the office.

Politically, Clinton has not always been a Democrat. She was raised in a very conservative household and supported Republican candidate Barry Goldwater for president in 1964. During her college years, she was the president of the Wellesley Young Republicans and even attended the 1968 Republican National Convention. However, her political views began to change while in college, largely because of her opposition to the Vietnam Conflict. By 1976, she had become a staunch Democrat, working as Jimmy Carter's campaign director in Indiana.

Hillary Clinton announced she was running for president on April 12, 2015. She faced strong opposition from rival Bernie Sanders during the 2016 Democratic Primaries but ultimately succeeded in securing her party's nomination. On July 28th, 2016, Hillary Clinton accepted the Democrat nomination for president. With this nomination, she became the first woman to be the presidential nominee for either of the two main political parties in the United States.

On November 8, 2016, Hillary Clinton was defeated by Donald Trump in the 2016 presidential election. She acquired 65.8 million votes in this election. This was more than Trump's 62.9 million votes. However, Trump prevailed in the Electoral College vote by a count of 304 to 227. Despite the loss, her candidacy will remain important for its role in shattering barriers for future women who hope to hold elected office.

Donald J. Trump

Donald Trump is the Republican nominee for president. Who is Donald Trump? What are some of his major accomplishments in life?

Donald Trump was born on June 14th, 1946, in Queens, one of the five boroughs of New York City. His mother, Mary, was a homemaker, while his father, Fred, was a real estate developer. At the age of 13, Donald was enrolled at the New York Military Academy which he attended throughout his junior high and high school years.

After graduating high school, Trump attended Fordham University, a small private college in New York City. He then attended the Wharton School of Finance and Commerce at the University of Pennsylvania. In 1968, he received a bachelor's degree in Economics from Wharton. While still in college, Trump began his career in real estate. He assumed control of a failing apartment complex which his father had purchased in 1962. Through Trump's efforts, the complex became successful, and the Trump Organization sold it in 1972 for $6.75 million.

Donald Trump was involved in many construction and real estate development projects throughout the early 1970s. Many of these projects were intended to offer housing for middle class families in the New York City area, as well as other major cities. The Trump Organization was also responsible for the construction of the Grand Hyatt Hotel in 1978 and Trump Tower in 1983. Trump Tower is a 58 story skyscraper in Manhattan, which includes offices, residences, shops, and restaurants. (Trump Tower is not to be confused with Trump World Tower, a 72 story building which was completed in 2001).

As Trump's success in real estate continued to grow, he branched out into other business endeavors. In 1984, he opened a casino, Harrah's at Trump Plaza, in Atlantic City, New Jersey. Four years later, he took over the construction of another casino, the Taj Mahal Casino, which was completed in 1990.

Trump has had many other financial ventures, far too many to list in this lesson. Amongst the many items that Trump has licensed or endorsed include Trump Restaurants, Trump Drinks, Trump Magazine, Trump Chocolate, Trump Golf, Trump Steaks, and Trump Vodka. There is also a line of menswear, two different colognes, a television production company, a home furnishings company, and an online travel website which bear his name. There is even a board game, Trump: The Game, which was released in 1989. Many of these investments were financially lucrative, while others were not.

Donald Trump's financial net worth is difficult to estimate, largely because there is great discrepancy over the value of many of his real estate holdings. Some have estimated his value as low as $2.9 billion, while others claim it could be as high as $7 billion. However, Forbes Magazine, which produces a yearly list of the four hundred wealthiest people on the planet, has carefully estimated Trump's net worth at $4.5 billion in 2015. This figure ranked him as the 336th wealthiest person in the world.

Aside from his financial dealings, Donald Trump has also become a successful television personality. Throughout the 1980s and 1990s, he appeared in several movies, and numerous television programs, as "himself". In 2003, he became the host and executive producer of The Apprentice, a television program which aired on NBC. The show featured competitors battling for high-level management positions, with Trump deciding who won and lost, dismissing candidates with his catchphrase "You're fired!" Trump has been nominated for two Emmy Awards, and in 2007, he was given a star on the Hollywood Walk of Fame for his contributions to American television.

Throughout his business and television career, Trump married three times. The first marriage, to Ivana, and the second, to Marla Maples, both ended in divorce. He has been married to his third wife, Melania, since 2005. He has five children, Donald Jr., Ivanka, Eric, Tiffany, and Barron. He also has eight grandchildren.

Politically, Trump's views and affiliations have changed over the course of his life. In the late 1970s, he supported the presidential candidacy of Republican Ronald Reagan. He registered as a Republican in 1987 and remained a Republican until 1999, at which time he joined the Reform Party and briefly considered running for president as the Reform Party candidate. He then registered as a Democrat from 2001 to 2009, before rejoining the Republican Party in 2009. He has financially supported candidates from both parties throughout his career.

Donald Trump first considered running for president in 1988. He was also briefly considered as a vice presidential running mate for George H.W. Bush that same year. He also explored the idea of running for president in both 2004 and 2012. In 2006, and again in 2014, he briefly considered the possibility of running for Governor of New York.

Trump officially announced his candidacy for president on June 16, 2015. He became one of sixteen Republican candidates in what was thought to be a very strong field. During the 2016 Republican Primaries, Trump won early and decisive victories in New Hampshire, South Carolina, and Nevada. As other candidates bowed out of the contest, Trump faced his most staunch opposition from Texas Senator Ted Cruz. Throughout the primary season, Trump acquired nearly 14 million votes. This was a record for the most primary votes in the history of the Republican Party.

On July 21st, 2016, Donald Trump officially accepted the Republican Party's nomination for president. On November 8, 2016, Donald J. Trump won the 2016 presidential election against Hillary Clinton. He achieved this victory by winning 304votes in the Electoral College to Clinton's 227 Electoral College votes.

On January 20, 2017, Trump was inaugurated as the 45th President of the United States. With his victory, Trump became the first U.S. President with no prior political or military experience. He is also the wealthiest person to ever hold the office of the presidency.

President Donald Trump meeting with
North Korean Supreme Leader, Kim Jong-un.

About the Author:

Jake Henderson is a graduate of Southwestern Oklahoma State University in Weatherford, OK, where he earned a BA in History Education. He also has a Master's Degree in History Education from SWOSU, which he earned in 2004. He has taught US History, World History, AP Government, US Government, Geography, Oklahoma History, and Psychology at the High School level for more than fifteen years. Jake has also authored several fiction books including *Ryan's Crossing*, *Original Spin*, *Radio Road*, *A Radio Road Christmas*, and *Radio Road: Summer Games*. He currently lives and teaches in Woodward, OK.

Made in the USA
Middletown, DE
21 June 2019